The Dubs

DUBLIN GAA SINCE THE 1940S

Other works by the Author:

BOOKS

Sean Óg — His Own Story

The Birth of a Building

History of Hermitage Golf Club: Celebrating 100 Years (1905 to 2005)

Tall Tales and Banter

My Greatest Sporting Memory

PLAYS

A Scent of Hawthorn

A Man from the Island

RADIO PLAYS

An Braon Searbh

Aedín agus an Cailleach

VIDEO

History of Hermitage Golf Club

The Dubs

DUBLIN GAA SINCE THE 1940S

SEÁN ÓG Ó CEALLACHÁIN

GILL & MACMILLAN

Contents

Seán Ó Ceallaigh

Teachtaireacht an Uachtaráin

Seán Ó Ceallaigh
UACTHARÁN CLGG 2002–6

Is chuis mór áthas dom an alt seo a scríobh ar fhoilsiú an leabhar iontach seo, ag féachaint siar ar stair Chumann Luthchleas Gael i mBaile Átha Cliath.

The publication of this much needed and eagerly awaited tome will be greeted with enthusiasm by GAA followers everywhere, but most particularly by followers of our games in the capital city. The book is an excellent reflection on how the fortunes of Gaelic games have ebbed and flowed in Dublin from the days of my fellow Kerryman, Joe Fitzgerald (who captained the Dubs in the 1942 All-Ireland football final), and the great names of that era such as Bobby Beggs, Peter O'Reilly and Brendan Quinn, right up to the modern Dubs and the wall of blue that is Hill 16.

There were also, of course, the glorious hurling years of the 1940s, 50s and 60s when Áth Cliath featured in no less than six All-Ireland finals, or the football memories of Heffo, 'Snitchie' Ferguson, the Foleys and Simon Behan, and of course those wonderful and colourful September Sundays of the 1970s, when Keaveney, Hanahoe, Doyle and McCaul were the biggest draws in town.

As chairman of the Strategic Review Implementation committee, I see the production of such an informative and interesting publication as adding greatly to the overall drive to promote our games in the city. There are many people throughout Dublin working tirelessly in schools and clubs to promote Gaelic games. I have no doubt that one day the fruits of their efforts will be commemorated in print in the manner in which this book reflects on the past glories of Dublin GAA and the men who made it.

The author's own contribution to the success of the GAA in Dublin is also most noteworthy. The younger generation recognises the dulcet tones of Seán Óg from his wonderful radio results service on Radio Éireann every Sunday night. They may be surprised to hear, however, that he has been keeping GAA followers up to date in this fashion since January 1953 — an incredible record by any standards — and that his father performed the same duty from as far back as 1930.

They may be even more surprised to hear that Seán Óg himself was a renowned hurler and footballer and played for many years in the blue of Dublin in both codes, featuring at left half forward on the Dublin team that contested the 1948 All-Ireland hurling final against Waterford. Seán Óg scored a goal on that occasion and I would venture that for a man whose memories are so wide and varied this particular nugget must elicit a happy smile. That he refereed an All-Ireland minor final, an Ulster senior football final and an All-Ireland senior football semi-final is just further proof of the outstanding talent of this great man.

I would like to wish Seán Óg every success with this terrific publication, and I sincerely hope that you, the readers, enjoy the read and the trip down memory lane as much as I have.

Réamhrá

Séamus de Grae
DUBLIN COUNTY BOARD CHAIRMAN 1968–80

That Seán Óg is unique in the world of the GAA is to understate his contribution to the promotion of Gaelic games down the years. My fond recollection is of his father Seán Senior, who gave out the GAA results on the radio every Sunday night, and when my brothers and I went on summer holidays to Longford, our house would be packed with people anxiously listening to the GAA results of the day.

Then one night Seán Óg Ó Ceallacháin was introduced as the presenter and there was considerable debate as to whether this was a gag of some sort, because the voice sounded the same. Seán Óg is and was a great defender of the Dubs, particularly in the 70s when, if ever there was criticism of the players, his column in the *Evening Press* jumped to their defence. Indeed, he played a part in the appointment of Kevin Heffernan as Dublin team manager. He relates this in the book and, given the eventual outcome for Dublin and the GAA, he can take great satisfaction for his part in the whole affair.

Seán is a very good friend of mine, not alone since my terms as Dublin and Leinster council chairman, but also as a former player with the county. I thoroughly enjoyed this excellent book. I found his mix of GAA history and politics in the years under review educational, intriguing and enlightening.

Séamus de Grae, Dublin County Board Chairman, 1968–80

*Micheál Ó Dúbhshiláine
Secretary, Leinster Council GAA*

Réamhrá

Micheál Ó Dúbhshláine

SECRETARY, LEINSTER COUNCIL GAA

Writing in his annual report to the 1945 Leinster convention, secretary Martin O'Neill wrote of Dublin: 'We record our deep appreciation of their county teams who in the present emergency have travelled to all venues arranged by the Leinster Council. Despite all the attractions, a Dublin championship game has big public patronage which is growing year by year by reason of the excellence of the teams.'

Sixty years on, the same sentiments can be expressed — witness the 2005 Leinster senior football final when an all-time record of over 82,000 patrons were present in Croke Park. With all due respect to my native Laois, I have to acknowledge that at least 75 per cent of that attendance was there to support Dublin.

What does Dublin mean to Leinster and, by extension, to the GAA at large? It means glamour, colour, atmosphere, entrenched views, whiffs of controversy, and healthy financial returns. Hill 16 in full voice and draped in sky blue and navy — especially on a big Leinster championship day — is a spectacle which cannot be replicated in any sporting arena in the world. Is it (the Hill) an advantage to the Dubs? Perhaps it is, but should we begrudge them that?

Units of the GAA such as the Leinster Council depend solely on gate receipts to implement our development programmes, be they facilities or in the area of game promotion. When Dublin are going well they represent a virtual ATM for the GAA. I have worked with Dublin and the Dubs since the mid-70s, witnessing the highs and lows of the last 30 years. From the time of Heffo's heroes to the current squad, the Dublin senior football team has rarely been too far from the top.

When a dip in interest in the GAA threatened in the early 90s, what happened? Along came that never to be forgotten four-game saga of 1991 between Dublin and Meath. That put the GAA back on the front pages and gave the Leinster council the wherewithal to implement ambitious physical developments in the province — such as Parnell Park, Portlaoise, Kilkenny and Carlow — as well as the major coaching initiatives now active in all our 12 counties.

Love them or loathe them, the Dubs are one of our greatest assets in Leinster.

Long may it continue to be so.

Tommy Moore (1891–1973). He joined Faughs in 1911 and went on to become one of the major figures in Dublin hurling circles at both club and county level, winning six senior championships and seven senior hurling leagues with Faughs and four Leinster senior championships and two All-Irelands with Dublin. He was chairman of the club from 1929 to 1969, then president from 1969 to his death in 1973.

(Watercolour portrait by Pat McGilloway)

Pat Farrell (1896–1980). First player and eventually secretary of Faughs, a position he held up to 1969, he also represented the club at Dublin County Board meetings. He was chairman of the Dublin Junior Board in 1934 and 1935 and was a Dublin senior hurling selector for many years.

(Watercolour portrait by Pat McGilloway)

PREFACE

The purpose of this book is to dwell primarily on the successes and otherwise of Dublin football and hurling teams during and since World War II. A little background covering that period may be essential. This will enable the reader to appreciate the difficulties which faced the GAA, the country's largest sporting organisation. It may also show a picture, however briefly, of how this country faced, as a nation, one of the greatest challenges in its history. The 1940s, which will provide the starting point, proved significant in their own way. In 1940 the GAA had 1,718 affiliated clubs and, despite food shortages and petrol restrictions, the association's finances were in a reasonably sound position. The start of the championships in May coincided with the launch by the German Army of a major offensive on the western front. By the end of June the Germans had overrun Holland, Belgium and France, and by July they controlled the entire western coastline of Europe from the tip of Norway to the Spanish frontier. Irish neutrality had been declared by Taoiseach Éamon de Valera and was respected, but the country faced grave economic problems. Ireland was cut off from her main source of supply, ships were scarce and shipping lanes hazardous, to say the least. The government set up the Local Defence Force (LDF) to assist the regular army, the Local Security Force (LSF) to assist the Gardaí, and the ARP which was to deal with the fall-out of a possible air raid attack.

In 1941 everyone was feeling the effects of the 'Emergency', as we in this part of the island euphemistically called it. There was little or no coal: turf and wood were the main fuels. They provided the furnace fire for the infrequent running of trains. Tea was rationed to half an ounce per person. I was then a member of the LSF until an event happened which made me change over to the LDF under army control. On the night of 31 May, a fortnight after my 18th birthday, a German bomber dropped three bombs in the vicinity of the North Strand on Dublin's northside not far from Croke Park, killing 37 and injuring many. The huge bomb which had fallen at 2.08 a.m. on the North Strand Road, on the city side of Newcomen Bridge, had caused appalling devastation which I will never forget.

There was an ironic twist to that awful happening which concerned my football club, O'Tooles, related to me by the club historian, Jimmy Wren, and told to him by the late Seán Synnott. Since being reformed in 1938, the hurling section of the club had no base from which to operate and gather together except for weekly meetings in Canavan's hairdresser's shop in Amiens Street. (Because of a dispute between the footballers and the hurlers, the latter were not allowed to use the club premises at 100 Seville Place.) In the early 1940s the hurlers succeeded in renting a basement room in a three-storey house on the main North Strand Road, beside Newcomen Bridge. The owner was an elderly lady who lived upstairs and who let the basement for two to three nights per week between the hours of 8 p.m. and 11 p.m. In this room was a half-size snooker table. On the fateful Friday night of the Whit bank holiday weekend of 1941, seven or eight of the O'Tooles hurlers and a few friends had their usual game of snooker and at 11 p.m. locked the room, gave the keys to the owner and went home.

Two hours later the house was demolished by the bomb, which exploded almost directly in front of the house, and the elderly lady was killed instantly. The odd thing about the whole affair was that none of the lads seemed to realise that if the bomb had fallen two hours or so earlier, they would all have been killed. Their only concern was for the unfortunate owner. You could safely say that O'Tooles Hurling Club was only two hours or so from being completely wiped out.

When I passed the spot where that old house had stood early on that Saturday morning to take up duty with my LSF unit, a blazing gas pipe on the brow of the hill on Newcomen Bridge lit up the whole sky as I rushed from my home in Fairview to join all the people heading in that direction. It was Dublin's first real taste of the horror of war.

On the GAA front, Pádraig McNamee was again re-elected president, a significant honour for the first Ulsterman to hold this prestigious position. The association was to face other major problems which were to occur with the introduction of severe travel restrictions, and worse still, the spread of the foot-and-mouth epidemic which applied to cattle and sheep. The three counties worst hit were Carlow, Kilkenny and Tipperary. Arrangements had to be made to prevent the spread of the disease at all pitches throughout the land. The GAA fixtures committee, in an attempt to straighten out the schedule of matches, took a bold step. The All-Ireland football final was brought forward to the first Sunday in September and the hurling final was relegated to the third Sunday. As the GAA history books recall at the time, the All-Ireland junior championships in hurling and football were cancelled, and they were not to be resumed until after the war. That also applied to the national leagues, which were also abandoned because of the unavailability of trains or other means of transport, due to lack of fuel.

Remarkably, the Railway cup matches in Croke Park on St Patrick's Day still attracted an attendance of 21,187. The Munster football team which defeated Ulster included all the great Kerry stars of that era, Joe Keohane, Bill Myers, Bill Casey, Paddy Kennedy, and Cork's Eamon Young. Leinster beat Munster in the hurling encounter, but Christy Ring had to wait until 1942 before making his Railway cup debut.

Although the war had a significant effect on the lives of people, and sports events were very much curtailed, with a drastic falling off in attendance at GAA matches, Dublin wasn't hindered too much in that respect.

Seán Óg Ó Ceallacháin

The War Years (1939–45)

As a former Dublin player, both hurling and football, I am privileged and thankful to have lived through the period which dictated my thoughts when I commenced writing this book. The strengths and weaknesses of Dublin in this particular survey can only be measured on the basis of the premier titles won, both in football and hurling. Undoubtedly, football commanded far greater success in that regard. Hurling trails very much in the footballer's slip-stream. It is 67 years since Dublin last won the coveted Liam McCarthy All-Ireland trophy. On that occasion only one Dublin-born player, Jim Byrne from my own club Eoghan Ruadh, figured on that 1938 winning team.

The war years affected the GAA very much, not alone the staging of games but also the restrictions on travel which denied them the support those games normally attracted. Looking at the attendance figures for the meeting of such great rivals as Dublin and Kerry in the 1941 All-Ireland football semi-final (drawn game 16,000, replay 15,000) these figures pale very much in comparison with subsequent clashes.

Although Galway and Kerry played before 45,000 in the All-Ireland final that year, the All-Ireland hurling finalists,

Dublin and Cork, brought only 26,000 to Croke Park. That could be attributed to the absence of transport but also the cursed foot-and-mouth disease. The worst ever outbreak of the dreaded cattle and sheep epidemic brought sporting activities in Ireland to a complete standstill, particularly in Munster. Only south Leinster felt the blow, denying Kilkenny any participation in the hurling championship.

It led to a unique situation. The provincial councils of Leinster and Munster nominated Dublin and Cork as the All-Ireland finalists that year, even though neither of the two counties had won its provincial title. An effort was made to postpone the hurling final further because of the close-down of hurling by the foot-and-mouth scourge, but it failed. The Central Council of the GAA moved quickly to prevent any more objections and laid down the law: teams nominated to contest All-Ireland finals would fulfil that engagement and the winning team would be awarded the All-Ireland title. In the case of the Dublin and Cork match, it proved a very one-sided affair. Cork cantered away with the game on a 5-11 to 0-6 scoreline. When the cattle restrictions were finally lifted later that year, the belated Munster final between Tipperary and Cork was played, and Cork (the then All-Ireland champions) were comfortably beaten 5-4 to 2-5. Efforts by Tipperary to claim the premier title were immediately shot down by president Pádraig McNamee and the Central Council. Naturally there were murmurings in the Premier county about Cork 'stealing our rightful title', but that was the end of it. But not for Cork. It was the start of a Cork rampage which was to yield an unparalleled run of All-Ireland successes in hurling and football.

The fact that most counties depended on grants from the association brought it quickly to mind that revenue from that source was going to dry up sooner rather than later. There was no doubt the effects of the foot-and-mouth disease, coupled with the restriction on travel, hit deeply. That situation was not relieved until late in November that year when the cattle and sheep disease threat began to abate. The financial returns from provincial field games was very poor. That was reflected at Congress in 1942 when the GAA reported one of the leanest financial returns for many years.

Over a dozen or so of the more prominent strongholds of the national games were very badly hit and that applied at the very important championship period of the year. Munster and Leinster could not complete their championship programmes to provide the necessary All-Ireland semi-finalists for the normal August schedule. Hence the decision was taken to nominate the teams to contest the relevant All-Ireland finals. Leinster staged their football championship programme in 1941. Dublin reached the Leinster senior football final for the first time since 1934. Their opponents in the final were Carlow, who had reached the decider for the first time in their history. Chosen at midfield for Dublin was Con Martin (Air Corps) whom I had played against in my schooldays with Coláiste Mhuire. Con was the star of St Vincent's CBS Glasnevin teams in hurling and football. But he was also an all-rounder when he joined the Air Corps, being proficient not alone at hurling and football but also at soccer and basketball. He caught the Dublin selectors' eyes following displays in the county championships. He played a leading role when partnering Joe Fitzgerald of Geraldines at midfield against Carlow in the Leinster final played on 9 November that year. Naturally, no function feted Dublin on their provincial success and Con was lucky to catch the last bus back to Baldonnel. He was deposited at Clondalkin and had to walk to his base at Baldonnel Aerodrome carrying his football gear. Army Air Corps had no 'bans' on sport; their members could play all the games they wished. But when it was learned that Con had been playing soccer with Drumcondra, the infamous 'foreign games' rule came into the equation. When the Dublin county board distributed the Leinster final medals, Con Martin's medal

The 1938 hurling final, Dublin v Waterford, as it looked from the Canal end.

was withheld because of the ban rule. However, 40 years later he received his medal. Long before that Con had become one of Ireland's greatest soccer stars, a legendary player north and south. He didn't gain his place the following year when Dublin retained the Leinster title, beating a very impressive Carlow team. By that time Con was committed to playing soccer.

Matters worsened early in 1942 when the government decided to withdraw all petrol rations for motorists. Sunday bus services stopped altogether throughout the country. The GAA consequently abandoned the junior and minor championships until normality was restored. The senior grade got an unexpected boost, and where there was access to games unaffected by travel restrictions, attendances very much improved.

An exceptional year for Dublin was 1942 when the county qualified for both the All-Ireland senior hurling and football finals, a feat never previously accomplished, nor indeed since. Adding further to that rare achievement, Paddy 'Beefy' Kennedy played in both finals, at full back for the footballers and full forward for the hurlers. He had mixed luck on the medal front. He was a winner in football and a loser in hurling. Admittedly, Dublin were not given the remotest chance of beating Cork in the hurling final, following their disastrous defeat the previous year in the final.

On the political front the Emergency Powers Act 1939 (EPA) gave the Irish Government a range of extraordinary powers deemed necessary for securing public safety, the preservation of the State, the maintenance of public order, and the provision and control of essential supplies and services. This was licence to rule by decree and the normal legislative functions of parliament were suspended.

But the effects of the government's policy of withdrawing petrol coupons increased the country's appetite for action on the inter-county front. Cork were hell bent on retaining their McCarthy cup against Dublin in the 1942 All-Ireland hurling final. Dublin only included four of the side which failed to measure up to Cork the previous year. Newcomer at full forward was Beefy Kennedy, who had the unique distinction of being chosen on the All-Ireland football team later against Galway.

A feature of the 1941 winning Cork team was the inclusion of a young rising star, Christy Ring, making his All-Ireland senior debut. The only consolation for Dublin was their win over Kilkenny in the belated Leinster final, which was played on 2 November at Croke Park. Dublin retained their Leinster senior title by beating Kilkenny 4-8 to 1-4. While the Dublin teams of that era were dominated by players drawn from the other hurling strongholds, the number of Dublin-born players on the 1942 selection had risen to five. Cork beat Galway in the All-Ireland semi-finals by the narrow margin of two points, and on 6 September they again put paid to Dublin on a 2-14 to 3-4 scoreline. Christy Ring was one of the leading marksmen for Cork. Jack Lynch, their captain, went on to achieve an unbelievable six All-Ireland medals on the trot, which included an All-Ireland senior football medal in 1945, winning his 6th All-Ireland title with the Cork hurlers in 1946.

Following the fall of France in 1940, fear of invasion gripped the country and Fine Gael privately suggested to the Fianna Fáil government that neutrality should be abandoned. It proposed an All-Ireland defence system consisting of British, French and Irish troops, under overall French command, as a pre-emptive move against a German invasion. Fine Gael leader W. T. Cosgrave privately intimated to Éamon de Valera that if the government felt the need to abandon neutrality, it would have his party's fullest support. De Valera, in reply, stressed the government's belief that neutrality offered the best hope of preserving the State from invasion. For the remainder of the war Fine Gael fully supported neutrality as the only game in town. James Dillon spoke out against it in the

Dáil in July 1941 and again at the party's Árd Fheis in February 1942 (following the entry of the US into the war in 1941). His reward was forced resignation from Fine Gael and isolation.

On the playing fields, predictably, attendances were dropping at an alarming rate, which was of the utmost concern to the GAA. That was very much reflected in the returns from the Munster senior hurling final between old rivals, Cork and Tipperary, when only 24,000 watched the Leesiders take the honours by 4-15 to 4-1. Once again the prime support came from the loyal supporters who trudged, cycled or used pony and trap to attend the game. The provincial bodies soon caught on and when fixtures were arranged, they paired neighbouring counties in a bid to secure much needed finance and less travelling distances for the supporters. It must be said that, in spite of wartime conditions, the crowds attending GAA games were truly amazing.

Another distinguishing feature was the increase in local entertainment, and ballads made a come-back. 'Kelly the Boy from Killane', and 'Boolavogue' were revived in Wexford. The 'Bard of Armagh' was heard in the north-east and 'Carrigdhoun' in the south-west. One of the most popular was 'Jack Duggan, the Wild Colonial Boy', who was born in Castlemaine. The Abbey

The 1938 hurling team. BACK ROW, LEFT TO RIGHT: *Harry Gray, Bobby Ryan, Jack Gilmartin, Pat Doody, Tom Teehan, Art Murphy, Mick Flynn, Jim Donegan, Charlie McMahon.* MIDDLE ROW, LEFT TO RIGHT: *Jim Byrne, Phil Farrell, Mick Butler, Mick Daniels, Charley Downes, Paddy Brophy, Paddy McCormack, Christy Forde.* FRONT ROW, LEFT TO RIGHT: *Larry Hayes, Mossie McDonnell, Mick Gill, Bill Loughnane, Dave Hurley, Dessie O'Brien.*

Theatre staged Gaelic pantomimes and plays by O'Casey and Michael Murphy. The theatres were packed and did a roaring business.

Galway and Dublin won their way to the All-Ireland football final in 1942. The previous year Kerry had beaten Dublin in the All-Ireland semi-final replay in Tralee. On the way down by train to the Kerry venue that morning, the Dublin train ran out of fuel and Peter O'Reilly and some of the Dublin players had to chop up wood to enable the train to reach Tralee station. Kerry went on to beat Galway in the All-Ireland final that year. In 1942, Dublin beat Cavan in the semi-final and

Galway also atoned for the previous year's set-back against Kerry by narrowly beating the holders 1-3 to 0-3.

Nine Dublin-born players lined out against Galway for that All-Ireland final, including Bobby Beggs, who had played for Galway the previous year. Beggs, a fisherman and native of Skerries, Co. Dublin, declared for the county for the 1942 All-Ireland final. Craggy Bobby Beggs was a tower of strength all through the championship series, but never were his services more needed than against the Galwaymen in that pulsating final. It was sensational stuff played before an attendance of 37,000 (gate receipts

£2,635). The closing five minutes of that match were heart palpitating as Dublin held on tenaciously to a one-point lead. Galway were awarded a 50 to be taken by ace free taker Joe Casey. Dublin followers held their breath and the stadium was hushed as Casey squared up to the ball. Four minutes remained on the clock on that sunlit afternoon on 20 September 1942. Four minutes to survive and Dublin would be All-Ireland champions after a lapse of 19 years. The metropolitans would equal Kerry's 15 championship wins.

Casey's kick soared straight for the Dublin uprights. As it fell, six men took off in unison — six groping pairs of hands probed the skies. But one man went higher than the rest. As he came charging out of the ruck, ball held tightly to his chest, the sturdy frame of 'man of the match' Peter O'Reilly shook off all efforts to prevent him clearing the ball. But clear it he did. True to their nature the Galwaymen rallied, and only great defensive work by Bobby Beggs, Beefy Kennedy, Caleb Crone, Brendan Quinn and the unstoppable Peter O'Reilly foiled gallant Galway of a draw. A last-minute point from corner forward Matt Fletcher gave the home county victory by 1-10 to 1-8. It was football at its very best. The two teams rose to the occasion in rare style and there

Dublin Leinster senior football championship 1940. BACK ROW: P. Toolan (Parnells), Tom Jenkinson (O'Tooles), Gerry McLoughlin (Ben Eaders), P. Dowling (Pioneers), Mick Richardson (Pioneers), Brendan Quinn (Parnells), Matt Fletcher (Peadar Mackens). FRONT ROW: H. Donnelly (Fingallians), Peter O'Reilly (St Mary's), M. O'Reilly (Parnells), Paddy Bermingham (St Mary's), Ignatius Levey (Geraldines), Paddy Mulhall (St Joseph's), Patsy Power (Parnells), Gerry Fitzgerald (St Mary's).

were brilliant passages of high-powered football. The pity was that one team had to lose. One aspect of Dublin's play which fascinated me was the sliding tackle indulged in by wing back Brendan Quinn. It proved a very effective method of nipping Galway attacks in the bud. Donegal referee Seán Kennedy, one of the best at the time, obviously deemed it a legal challenge. I had great doubts myself of its legality.

Peter O'Reilly's contribution was really immense. Not alone did he dominate all before him at centre back, but he also took over the training of the team, an unparalleled feat at the time. Sport featured prominently in the O'Reilly family as Peter's brother, Joe, began making headlines in soccer. He won his first FAI cup medal with Brideville in 1927, and two years later he became one of the youngest players ever to win Irish international honours when he was capped at 19 years of age. There was an amusing sequel to the celebrations that marked Dublin's much-heralded victory in that 1942 All-Ireland final, and it is worth including in this survey. It concerned Beefy Kennedy.

By tradition the GAA was wedded to a Spartan culture. Up until the 1960s club grounds with running water and sanitation were the exceptions. But it has to be said that these facilities were the exception in many parts of rural Ireland too in those days. By the same token, recreational buildings up to the 1950s were subject to a statutory maximum outlay of £750, due to the shortage of building materials in the wake of World War II. Today, recreation throughout society at home and abroad has become a major industry. Players in traditionally professional games are traded in millions, where previously a few thousand pounds was the going rate. Quite recently Rugby Union, by tradition a bastion of the amateur culture, has gone professional. Down the years, in the rugby ethos, a player who turned to the professional game could never again be admitted to the amateur ranks as a player; nor was he eligible for membership of an amateur club once his playing days were over. The GAA, apart from its notorious ban on foreign games, had its social norms too. Until after World War II ladies were in practice excluded from the festive table. But it has to be said that they always enjoyed parity of esteem at the turnstiles. Up until wartime 'smoking concerts' were a feature of male recreation in the GAA. A group would book a large room in a hotel for a social gathering laced with drink and song. Smoking concerts disappeared early during wartime; rationing saw to that. By the way, medical knowledge regarding the health hazards of smoking was in the womb of time at that point.

May I now refer to a social function organised by the Dublin county board that ran amok, cost-wise. The occasion was the celebration dinner to honour the Dublin footballers' All-Ireland success of 1942. Nineteen years had elapsed since a previous win by the footballers in 1923. It was a particularly good year for the county, and it was decided that the hurlers, beaten by Cork, would also partake in the occasion which took place in November. In keeping with the culture of the day, it was an exclusively male presence, apart from the waitresses.

The celebration, which was confined to the teams and officials, took place in Clery's, O'Connell Street. It was a very enjoyable affair despite the wartime restrictions. Treasurer of the county board at the time was Tom Woulfe, and his Civil Service colleague Seán Ó Braonain was county chairman. The county board supplied the drink at the dinner, but because of rationing no whiskey was served. Guinness stout was the order of the day.

At around 11.30 p.m. Woulfe was approached by Beefy Kennedy, the player who had figured in both All-Ireland finals that year, who said the Guinness had run out. Woulfe set off to inform Ó Braonain. Ó Braonain took out his notebook and tore a leaf from it. He surveyed the crowd and wrote an order for the storeman to supply a further 12 dozen stout to the tables. At that stage there were still about ninety people at the function. Beefy offered to take the written order to Clery's storeman, whose job it was to look after such details. As the chairman, a strict teetotaller, was leaving the festivities around 12.30 a.m., he couldn't but fail to

The Dublin team that beat Galway 1-10 to 1-8 in the 1942 All-Ireland final. BACK ROW, LEFT TO RIGHT: *Tommy McCann, Sean Healy, Paddy Henry, Tommy Banks, Colm Boland, Charlie Kelly, Paddy 'Beefy' Kennedy, Brendan Quinn, Joe Delaney, Matt Fletcher, Mick Richardson, Bobby Beggs, Frank Ryan.* FRONT ROW, LEFT TO RIGHT: *Peter O'Reilly, Paddy Birmingham, Caleb Crone, Joe Fitzgerald, Paddy O'Connor, Gerry Fitzgerald, Mick Falvey, Johnny Joy, Sean Moriarty.*

observe the behavioural transformation throughout the room that the extra bottles of stout had caused. A sedate gathering had become a rollicking party in no time. He mused aloud that perhaps he was witnessing a repeat of the 'Miracle of Cana'.

A month later, when the bill for the function arrived from Clery's, the drink item was staggering. Woulfe knew that Beefy had changed the 12 dozen to 72 dozen stout. The party was still going strong at 4 in the morning. The chairman was furious when he saw the cost of the drink and challenged Woulfe about it. Tom responded that he only transmitted the order as instructed. Woulfe claimed later that he applied the old Chinese proverb to delicate situations: 'Those who don't know don't talk and those who don't talk don't know.' It was a bloody great night, nevertheless!

The Freedom of Information Act allows the public access to information and records relating to the last war. It showed that Ireland was distinctly 'neutral for the British'. De Valera co-operated far more with the Allies than most people in Ireland or Britain had previously realised. During the blitz, de Valera offered refuge to British women and children. War records show that he protested publicly about Germany's invasion of Holland and Belgium in May 1940, despite Ambassador Hemple's complaints.

On the other hand, the Allies complained to the Irish Government about the existence of a radio transmitter in the German legation through which Hemple sent weather reports. Later in 1944, as preparations mounted for the invasion of Normandy, pressure was placed on Hemple to close down the transmitter as a danger to our neutrality. The weather issue cropped up also for my father, Seán Senior. He was told by the Radio Éireann authorities not to make any references to the weather in his Sunday night GAA reports of matches played that day. They said that radio programmes were being monitored by the Germans and that such weather information helped in the bombing of Britain.

America, like Ireland, was neutral, but our neutrality annoyed the Americans and pressure was again put on de Valera to change his position. When General Michael Costello of the Irish Army visited the States, America provided the Free State with 20,000 rifles to aid self-defence in case of a German invasion. Neither Britain nor the US was prepared to provide the weaponry which could help the Irish Free State defend the 'Treaty ports' against capture by Allied forces.

In late 1943, after the US had entered the war, David Gray, the US representative in Ireland who was deeply opposed to Ireland's neutrality policy, argued that the

States should demand air and port facilities in Ireland, and also that all Axis diplomats be removed from this country. American and British Notes were presented to the Irish Government on that matter in February 1944 and de Valera was very annoyed at what he saw as an infringement of our sovereignty. He replied coldly, pointing out Ireland's espionage successes and the fact that no foreign legation in the country was allowed to carry out intelligence activities. There was a huge wave of public support for the government, and Gray had to be given a police escort for a short while.

On the question of Irish neutrality the following piece, written by Captain Henry Harrison (ex British Army), responding to an article on Irish neutrality in the *New York Times* 1943, stated:

[Russia and America] were no voluntary crusaders leaping into the arena in unreflecting and disinterested enthusiasm for high moral principle. They had made no move when others were wantonly attacked. They remained neutral when Denmark and Norway, Holland and Belgium, Yugoslavia and Greece were in turn ravaged and enslaved. They fought because they had to, because they had no choice left, because they were attacked, because being attacked, they needs must fight or submit to a conqueror's yoke. And little Ireland was not attacked. That is the difference. That is the sole difference. For there is nothing more certain than that Ireland also would have fought back if she had been attacked.

It is also clear from the war records that Dublin and Britain benefited from Irish coast watchers who deliberately broadcast information on shipping movements, including submarines, to their regional commanders, who radioed them on to Dublin; Britain could then pick them up from there.

The GAA Congress 1943 reported that the association finances were in good shape for the previous year with income exceeding expenditure. A noted feature of the 1942 season was the decision by Congress to allow Ulster counties to compete in the senior ranks for the hurling championship. Antrim, playing in the 1943 series for the first time in 20 years, created a sensation by defeating not only Galway but also Kilkenny to qualify for their first senior final at Croke Park. Certainly their defeat of a highly fancied Kilkenny team stunned the hurling world. The Leinster champions paid a dear price for a rather nonchalant approach to a very important fixture. It was obvious that the black and amber brigade paid no heed to proper training for that visit to Belfast's Corrigan Park. They did have such household names as Paddy Grace, Paddy Larkin and Peter Blanchfield in defence, Jimmy Walsh at midfield, and such gifted hurlers as Jimmy Langton, Jimmy Kelly, Seánie O'Brien and Jack Mulcahy in attack. They didn't reckon on the unbelievable do or die spirit which backboned Antrim's mighty effort, fashioned by Jimmy Walsh, Noel Campbell, a beautiful hurler, Joe Butler, Johnny Bateman, Kevin Armstrong, a powerful dual player, and Seamie Mulholland. Antrim won the day beating the high-profile Kilkenny by 3-3 to 1-6. So it was on to Croke Park for the gallant Ulstermen and a date with the holders, Cork. Spectators travelling to that game used turf lorries, cattle trucks, push bikes and horse-drawn traps. Cork won the day easily by 5-16 to 0-4. The attendance was 48,843. Cork, the hurling team of the 1940s, remained top of the honours roll.

The winds of change were also blowing across the football scene. Dublin's dominance in Leinster was on the wane, and it would be 13 years before the city men would contest another All-Ireland football final. Dublin hurlers were faring no better. They won the Leinster championship in 1944, beat Antrim in the All-Ireland semi-final, but once again the might of Cork prevailed against them by 2-13 to 1-2. Though the Dublin teams at that time possessed excellent hurlers, Cork, with four victories on the trot at All-Ireland level behind them, were simply unbeatable.

New names hit the headlines in football in 1943 when the newly crowned Connacht champions, Roscommon, qualified to meet Cavan in the All-Ireland final. It was a unique pairing in one way without Kerry, the Munster kingpins, who had lost out to Cork in the Munster final that year. Roscommon, who had lost out to Galway in the 1941 and 42 Connacht deciders, came out with all guns blazing against their old rivals in the 1943 final to outplay and outmanoeuvre the holders by a decisive four-point margin to capture their first senior provincial crown. They went on to beat Leinster champions Louth in the All-Ireland semi-final. Cavan held them to a draw in the final, but Roscommon won the replay by a clear five-point margin.

Bonfires blazed all over the county heralding that first ever All-Ireland senior success. Roscommon had arrived as a football force and they were to prove it again the following year. A new face is always welcome despite the major threat from Kerry, who dominated the football scene from 1929 to 1932 and again, except for 1938 when they lost to Galway, from 1937 to 1941. The point forcibly made by Roscommon was the emergence of a new force captained by Knockcroghery's Jimmy Murray, his brother Phelim, Bill Carlos, Brendan Lynch, Liam Gilmartin, Donal Keenan and Jack McQuillan, to mention a few.

Séamus Gardiner of Tipperary took

over the role of president from Pádraig McNamee at the following Easter Congress. The war showed no sign of ending, and two days after the football final Seán Lemass, the Minister for Industry, put matters in perspective when he declared: 'Our main task now is to stay alive in a world where we have few friends.' He was relating to the war situation. Foodstuffs, clothes, gas and electricity were severely rationed. Imports were virtually non-existent and only cattle and people were exported to Britain. These emigrants took over jobs in munitions factories, and quite a few joined the British forces to fight the Germans.

All eyes were on Croke Park for the 1944 All-Ireland senior football final between Roscommon and Kerry, and it was to be a truly historic occasion. All records were broken by an attendance of 79,000. The gates at Croke Park had to be closed long before match time and many thousands had to stand around Jones's Road and Clonliffe Road. The residents in the area opened their windows so that the disappointed fans could at least listen to Michael O'Hehir's commentary on the match. It was perhaps the greatest hosting of people ever for an All-Ireland final in Dublin city. What made the occasion so remarkable was Roscommon's victory over the hotly fancied Kerrymen by two points.

It may be interesting to explain the historical background to the acquisition of Croke Park by the GAA. The stadium stands on land once known as Butterly's Field. The property of 21 acres and one rood was bought in 1864 by Maurice Butterly, who 30 years later sold it to a company called the City & Suburban Racecourse Amusement Ground. It was then used mainly for sports meetings and whippet racing and was frequently rented to the GAA, who first used it for the All-Ireland finals on 15 March 1896 (Tipperary v Meath and Tipperary v Kilkenny). In 1908 the property was bought by Frank B. Dineen, who was both general secretary and president of the GAA in the 1890s. He held it until such time as the association had sufficient funds. Eventually the GAA paid £3,641 to Dineen, and on 17 September 1914, GAA Utd was incorporated as the owner of the ground.

Hill 16 was put in place in 1917 with rubble from O'Connell Street (Dublin) in the aftermath of the 1916 Easter Rising. The Hogan stand commemorates Tipperary footballer Michael Hogan who was shot by British auxiliaries at Croke Park during a football challenge between Tipperary and Dublin on 21 November 1920, Bloody Sunday. It was ready for the first Tailteann Games in 1924. The Cusack stand was opened in 1938 and the Nally stand in 1952. The new Hogan stand was opened in 1959, a new Hill 16 in 1989 and the new Cusack stand in 1994. The construction of a new stand at the Canal end commenced in October 1998. Phase 3 of the redevelopment of the country's biggest stadium was completed with the erection of the new Hogan stand and the dismantling of the Nally stand, which allowed for a redeveloped Hill 16.

In 1901, a Thurles merchant sold 11 acres to the local Agricultural Show committee, who used this land for their various shows for nine years but then sold it to the GAA committee. It would be later named Semple Stadium after one of the committee members, Tom Semple, who had captained the Thurles Blues to win the 1906 and 1908 All-Ireland senior hurling championships. He also served as chairman of the Tipperary county board (1915 to 1917) as well as treasurer of the central council of the GAA. He was later president of the Thurles Sarsfields club before his death in April 1943. The first Munster hurling final played there was the 1914 decider between Cork and Clare with Tom Semple the referee. It was the first sportsfield to be singled out for redevelopment in the 1960s. It was later modernised with a new stand and terracing in time for the staging of the Centenary All-Ireland hurling final in 1984 between Cork and Offaly. The attendance was 59,814.

Roscommon's victory over Kerry in the All-Ireland final in 1944 was very significant. The Munster champions in their All-Ireland semi-final had to battle every inch of the way against a formidable Carlow team that had beaten Dublin to capture their first ever Leinster senior title, and Kerry considered themselves lucky to emerge victors by 3-3 to 0-10. The Kerry side had all their formidable stars: Danno Keeffe in goal, Tadgh Healy, Joe Keohane, Bill Dillon, Paddy Kennedy and Seán Brosnan at midfield, Jackie Lyne, Murt Kelly, and Paddy 'Bawn' Brosnan the captain at centre forward. Roscommon had sent a sharp message to Kerry when they hammered Cavan by 5-8 to 1-3 in their semi-final, but it took a little bit more effort to get the better of the mighty kingdom in the 1944 final.

During the later months of 1944 the shadow of war began to drift away from the western European seaboard. The new year brought no relief on the economic front; food remained scarce but we survived despite the restrictions. However, events were happening on the war front which gave rise to hopes of peace. In May 1945 the war with Germany came mercifully to an end. Then in August, America exploded atomic bombs which devastated Hiroshima and Nagasaki, and that horrific outcome brought the war with Japan to its conclusion.

The future development of Croke Park was very much on the mind of GAA

1944 Dublin All-Ireland senior hurling team. BACK ROW: *Ned Wade (Faughs) F. White, M. Ryan, M. Hassett, T. Flanagan, Terry Leahy (Faughs), Jim Egan (Faughs), Harry Gray (Faughs).* FRONT ROW: *J. Byrne, J. Donegan, Charlie Downes (Faughs,* CAPTAIN), *Mick Butler (Faughs), M. Maher, J. O'Neill, P. McCormack.*

Celebrating 100 years of All-Ireland winners. Dublin team representatives Seán Óg (1948), Mick Daniels (1938) and Noel Drumgoole (1961).

general secretary Pádraig Ó Caoimh and the association advertised for an architect to draw up a plan for the development of Croke Park. Ó Caoimh's 1945 report to Congress placed great emphasis on the affiliation of a record number of clubs (1,944), and finances were up on the previous year. President Séamus Gardiner was re-elected for another term. There were some interesting motions passed that year at Congress which were going to give football a major boost: the sideline kick was substituted for the throw-in from the hand; a move to abolish the hand pass just failed to get the necessary majority. A move to have an open draw in hurling was also beaten.

When All-Ireland football final time came round that year, Cork had replaced Kerry as the Munster champions. The prime topic of conversation was, would Jack Lynch capture a football winner's medal to add to his four successive hurling medals. The Cork team was a great side and they duly saw off the challenge of Cavan, who were still striving to win their third crown. Jack Lynch accomplished the notable feat of capturing that coveted All-Ireland football medal. Adding significantly to that occasion was the achievement of Eamon Young and Derry Beckett, two of Cork's best forwards. Their respective fathers, Jack Young and Jeremiah Beckett, were on the winning Cork team that beat Cavan in the 1911 All-Ireland final.

In 1946 Cork beat Kilkenny in the All-Ireland hurling final, which meant that Jack Lynch joined the ranks of the great by winning his sixth All-Ireland title in a row, five in hurling and one in football. That extraordinary feat has not been equalled since. Nor will it ever, in my humble opinion. The former taoiseach accomplished another extraordinary feat which was never properly highlighted or publicised. Some years before Jack's death, I was invited to appear on an 'Up for the Match' television programme which was paying a special tribute to Jack Lynch. I informed the programme producer about Jack's amazing and audacious achievement of playing three competitive matches on the one day — and scoring in all three. The producer told me to include it in my tribute to the brilliant Cork hurler, which I did.

On a Sunday morning in February 1944, I was captain of the Eoghan Ruadh hurling team which played Civil Service in an important senior hurling league game at Civil Service's own ground at Islandbridge. Much to my amazement, the goalkeeper was none other than Jack Lynch, the renowned Cork midfielder. It prompted me as the team's free taker to have a go for a goal from a 21 yard free. Though I hit the shot well, it was also well saved by goalkeeper Lynch. After that I concentrated on picking off points to ensure that Eoghan Ruadh would win and subsequently capture the league title. Jack moved outfield after the interval of that match and scored a few points, but our lead was never threatened. His appearance in that game intrigued me. I knew he had been chosen on the Munster football and hurling Railway cup semi-final teams for later that day at Croke Park.

I was present at GAA headquarters and watched both games that day. I saw Jack Lynch figure on the scoring returns in both matches, winning against Ulster in hurling but losing to Ulster in football. I can state categorically that Jack scored in all three matches that day in official competitions. I was to discuss that unique situation many years later with him when we met at a Civil Service function arranged in his honour.

I told Jack a story about Dermot O'Brien, the captain of the Louth football team for the 1957 All-Ireland final against Cork. Dermot told me the story for my *Evening Press* column some weeks after that final. Dermot had injured his shoulder in a local Louth football league match playing for his club, St Mary's, Ardee, some weeks before the All-Ireland semi-final against Tyrone. He was given extensive treatment for the shoulder, and a day before the Tyrone match his doctor ordered him to do some physical exercises like jumping for a ball and other tests. To Dermot's delight the shoulder injury had cleared up. The doctor was also pleased that the Ardee man's injury wasn't affecting him, but he told him that the

injury needed a longer healing period. Dermot played in his team's 0-13 to 0-9 victory, but at a crucial stage of that Tyrone game he got a shoulder in the chest after fielding the ball and was forced to retire. However, he was well and truly fit for the All-Ireland final against Cork, who had disposed of Galway in the other semi-final.

On the morning of the final in 1957, Dermot met his doctor in Dublin as he had arranged to get an injection for his shoulder as a precautionary measure. It meant that he didn't travel with the team to Croke Park, and when he arrived at the players' stile behind the Cusack Stand he found it closed up and the shutters down. He decided to walk around to the Hogan stand side of the stadium. When he got there, the stiles man said he couldn't admit him without his team ticket. Dermot pleaded with him and said he was the Louth captain. Still no joy. But a young Garda standing near by said to the gate man, 'Look, I can vouch for that man. He's the Louth team captain.' The gate man relented and Dermot was let through.

His next problem was to get to the dressing rooms on the Cusack Stand side of the pitch, which meant passing through a gate at the wire paling on the sideline. Dermot again explained his predicament to the gate man. No way, he was told, unless he had a team ticket. Despite Dermot's appeals, the gate man told him that he would lose his job if he allowed the

Louth man through. Hope arrived for Dermot when he saw a Cork official approaching, who he thought would vouch for him. He did not. As the Cork official had a ticket, he was allowed through the gate. It was getting close to match time and Dermot was now panicking. He heard a shout behind him from the spectators standing in front of the Hogan stand. The shout came from a friend of Dermot, Kevin Casey, a comedian and parody king. Dermot pointed to the gate and shrugged his shoulders. Casey, seeing his predicament, shouted, 'Let O'Brien through the gate.' The Louth followers took up the cry. Eventually it brought the necessary response from officialdom. The gate was opened and Dermot scurried across the pitch with the Louth supporters cheering him every inch of the way. When he got into the dressing room, there to meet him was the affable county chairman, Jimmy Mullen, with an anxious look on his face. 'What in the name of God kept you?' Dermot put up his hands. 'I'll tell you after the match. Let me get togged out.' Just over an hour later, Dermot was lifting up the Sam Maguire cup to the ringing cheers of the Louth supporters and a very happy Jimmy Mullen who had just watched his county win their third All-Ireland crown.

I digress. Back to Jack Lynch. He had a somewhat similar experience on the day of the 1945 All-Ireland senior football final against Cavan. It was more amusing than serious, but it still caused Jack a few heart flutters. Jack was living in Rathgar in Dublin and caught a bus to the city centre. He then took his place in a queue for another bus which would take him to the top of Clonliffe Road, beside Croke Park. The first bus to arrive was almost full and picked up just a few passengers. When a second bus arrived Jack was left stranded once again. As Jack went to get on board the third bus, he was stopped by the conductor who informed him that the bus was full. Jack pleaded with him and said he was playing in the All-Ireland for Cork in Croke Park and it was imperative that he get there on time. The conductor looked at him and started laughing. 'I've heard some good ones in my time but that bates the lot. Sorry, no room.' Jack eventually caught the next bus and arrived in the dressing room as the Cork team was about to take the field. Jim Barry, the trainer, who kept telling the selectors that Jack would make it, coldly said to him: 'I'm glad you thought of coming.'

But as the great hurler spoke to me about that game at that Civil Service dinner, he admitted: 'It won't go down as one of my best games in the Cork colours.' Derry Beckett's goal minutes from the end clinched Cork's 2-5 to 0-7 win over a gallant Cavan team, missing the inspirational presence of star forward Mick Higgins. Certainly but for sterling defensive play by Cavan's Simon Deignan, the Cork winning margin would have been greater. Cork's wing forward that day was Mick Tubridy, a Clareman who later declared for Clare. An army man and a superb member of the Irish equitation jumping team, he helped bring many honours to this country. The attendance was 67,329 (gate receipts £5,558).

The end of the war in Europe saw the beginning of normality in the working lives of the people country-wide. The tough emergency regulations were very much relaxed and GAA matches began to attract major support similar to pre-war days. Cork's 1945 success in the All-Ireland football final was their first for 35 years. Attendances at inter-county and provincial matches proved a highly welcome bonus for the association. The National Leagues in football and hurling made a welcome return, arousing all the old enthusiasm and support, and that was reflected in the record number attending the Railway cups on St Patrick's Day. Pádraig Ó Caoimh was lauded for his work in steering the association through its worst period in history. There were now 2,048 affiliated clubs, income had reached record levels (receipts for 1945 totalled £23,000), and the bank loan on Croke Park had been cleared.

Ireland's neutrality stance during the war posed a major challenge for the country and Éamon de Valera's Fianna Fáil-led government. The challenge lay in the decision to establish a credible working neutrality which appealed to both

1948 Dublin All-Ireland hurling final team. BACK ROW, LEFT TO RIGHT: *Paddy Donnelly, Seán Cronin, Joe Butler, Donal Cantwell, Davy Walsh, Ned Dunphy, Mick Hassett, Liam Donnelly, Gerry Sutton, Séamus Ó Ceallacháin, Des Dillon.* FRONT ROW, LEFT TO RIGHT: *Charley Kealy, Jimmy Kennedy, Kevin Matthews, Seán Óg Ó Ceallacháin, Tony Herbert, Frank Cummins* (CAPTAIN), *Jim Prior, Mick Williams, Joe Drumgoole, Aloysius Kealy.*

belligerents. To many external commentators with limited knowledge of the Irish situation and mentality at the time, this seemed improbable. Government thinking was captured in de Valera's own statement on the outbreak of the war: 'We, of all nations, know what force used by a stronger nation against a weaker one means.' Reading through the history of the emergency period, it was quite clear that de Valera maintained a very dignified position on Irish sovereignty and independence, to Britain's dismay.

It rankled in the mind of Winston Churchill in his victory speech to the world after the cessation of hostilities when he, albeit sarcastically, provided an opportunity for de Valera to express appreciation to the British prime minister for effectively resisting his overwhelming urge to invade Ireland. Churchill, as part of a self-congratulatory broadcast to the British on the defeat of Nazi Germany, had pronounced that the lack of access to the southern Irish bases had threatened to strangle Britain, but 'with a restraint and poise to which, I say, history will find few parallels, his Majesty's Government never laid a violent hand upon them, though at times it would have been quite easy and quite natural, and we left the de Valera government to frolic with the Germans and later with the Japanese representatives to their heart's content.'

Perhaps it should be pointed out that during long periods of the war the Irish Government kept supplying Britain with badly needed foodstuffs such as cattle and sheep. In 1943, when Britain refused to supply this country with wheat, the Free State threatened to stop exports of Guinness if we could not get enough wheat. At that time 80 per cent of beer supplies in Northern Ireland came from the Free State. Britain responded with an offer of 20,000 tons of wheat. Éamon de Valera still maintained his dignified approach in his reply to Churchill a few days later. During his broadcast, eagerly listened to by the Irish people, de Valera made allowances for Churchill's 'unworthy statement in the first flush of victory'. While he gave 'all credit to Churchill' for resisting the temptation to invade neutral Ireland, he then proceeded to attempt to explain the misunderstood Irish neutrality to Churchill:

Could he not find in his heart the generosity to acknowledge that there is a small nation that stood alone for not one year or two, but for several hundred years against aggression; that endured spoliation, famine, massacres in endless succession . . . a small nation that could never be got to accept defeat and has never surrendered her soul.

2

The Post-War Years

Extraordinary events occurred in the year 1946, both on and off the GAA fields. In Dublin the county hurlers were still battling for championship honours. I wasn't picked on the team to play Kilkenny in the Leinster final (I was among the subs), but an injury to Peadar Flanagan after 15 minutes gave me my chance. Dublin had enjoyed a very good start and I fired over a point immediately on taking the field.

A point from Ned Wade followed by a goal from Ned Daly and three great points from Tony Herbert left Dublin eight points clear. Kilkenny staged a great come-back and by half-time they had reduced the arrears to two points. The second half was a thriller with little between the two teams. A Tom Walton goal put Kilkenny ahead with minutes remaining. I still have vivid memories of those closing moments. I shot for a goal, but Kilkenny goalie Jim Donegan turned the ball round the post for a 70. Harry Grey lobbed the free to the square but Willie Walsh cleared the ball outfield for Kilkenny. Mick Gill (Dublin) gained possession and soloed towards the Kilkenny goal. He passed the ball to me. I moved forward a few paces and cracked a head high shot towards the Kilkenny posts, but the ball lifted in flight, struck the top of the crossbar and went over for a point.

7/2143352

A few inches lower and the game would have been drawn. My disappointment wasn't eased as I pushed through the crowd on the way to the dressing rooms, then behind the old Hogan stand, when a Dublin voice said, 'O'Callaghan should have gone for the goal.' I didn't look back.

Cork beat Kilkenny in the All-Ireland hurling final that year and Kerry beat Roscommon in the football final before an attendance of 75,771. That same year, 1946, saw the introduction of the Oireachtas cup and Corn Aghais for football and Antrim beat Laois in the final.

The 1946 weather became a bit of a nightmare not alone for the GAA but for the country at large. We had had a very wet summer and autumn, followed by an extremely harsh winter, with blizzards, heavy frost and intense cold, which brought most sporting events to a standstill. The GAA suffered very much. Most of their fixtures had to be cancelled. The National League programme was abandoned, and the Central Council decided to confine the closing stages to the counties leading their respective divisions.

In 1947 the St Patrick's Day fixture was confined to football in which Ulster beat Leinster. The hurling final was moved to Easter Sunday when Connacht beat Munster. But behind the scenes there were monumental decisions being discussed involving the New York GAA board and the Central Council. Congress was asked to decide on a request from New York to have the 1947 All-Ireland football final played in New York.

One of the men responsible for putting forward that idea was outgoing Clare county board chairman, Canon Michael Hamilton, the Irish representative of the New York Gaels. Not every county was enthusiastic about their eagerly looked forward to All-Ireland football final being exported to New York. It was thought that the decline of the national games in New York and other major GAA cities was proof that such a move would end in financial failure.

At Congress in 1947 the Clare motion was moved by Canon Hamilton. The stirring appeal made by the Clare cleric was met with instant approval. It was agreed that the general secretary Pádraig Ó Caoimh and Connacht council secretary Tom Kilcoyne would go to the States and make preliminary investigations into the prospect of such a venture. In the meantime, Congress ruled out a motion from Down to abolish the penalty for attending prohibited games. It was agreed that vigilance committees be again appointed, if necessary, to enforce the 'ban'.

Pádraig Ó Caoimh and Tom Kilcoyne returned from New York in mid-May and duly reported to the Central Council. A vote was taken and by 20 votes to 17 the council decided that the football final would be played in New York's Polo

Grounds, the Central Council having full control of the arrangements. The game was fixed for 14 September. Naturally, when this news was passed on, the effect it had on the football championship was really dramatic. Attendances grew and greater passion was infused into all of the games played. Meath beat Laois in Leinster; Roscommon retained their Connacht crown by defeating Sligo; Cavan took back the Ulster title against Antrim; and Kerry marched through Munster, beating Cork in the final.

In the All-Ireland semi-finals, Cavan beat Roscommon and Kerry saw off the challenge of Meath, so the finalists were Cavan and Kerry. Much work had to be done in the weeks and months before the staging of the All-Ireland final in New York's Polo Grounds. The Central Council succeeded in persuading the former president Pádraig McNamee to travel to New York ahead of Ó Caoimh. The Belfast teacher sacrificed his entire annual leave to take the secretary's place in putting the administrative machine in place in New York. He was delighted to get the full support of John Kerry O'Donnell, Mayor William O'Dwyer and members of the New York GAA board, who put their knowledge, experience and talents at McNamee's disposal.

It must be said that a considerable number of Central Council members at home were very much against the final being played in New York following Ó Caoimh's report after the trip to meet the New York officials. A motion from Waterford representative Vincent O'Donoghue (a future president of the GAA) to abandon the project was defeated by 20 votes to 17.

Dublin footballers had a lean spell following their defeat by Carlow in the 1944 Leinster final, and nine years were to elapse before they got back into the championship race. But the county hurlers were still holding their own against prime rivals, Kilkenny. The Dublin hurlers contested nine Leinster finals between 1939 and 1948, winning four titles. My brother Séamus and I were the first Dublin brothers to be chosen on the Leinster hurling team in 1947. It also included four other Eoghan Ruadh players, Seán Cronin, Ned Dunphy, Micky Banks and Jimmy Donegan, to make it the largest representation on the provincial team ever for the club. Connacht beat us in the Railway cup semi-final and then went on to beat Munster in the final to win their first ever provincial title. The 1947 All-Ireland final is still rated as the most thrilling and heart-stopping encounter ever played between those great rivals, Kilkenny and Cork. That game taught me a lesson I have never forgotten: never gamble on GAA matches.

I got involved that year in a situation which cured me for all time of the gambling urge. Con Murphy, a renowned rugby international full back and a

Corkman, persuaded me to accept a £10 bet on Cork to beat Kilkenny in that famous final. I was earning a little over a fifth of that per week at the time, so I decided to lay off part of the bet. I slipped into Tommy Moore's pub in Cathedral Street and asked Mick Butler, the manager and a former Kilkenny full back, if he would cover half the bet (£5). He told me that he had staked every penny he could muster on Kilkenny, and there was no way he could possibly place another penny on his native county. Indeed, he said, if Kilkenny were to lose that particular final, he would be working for his boss for the next six months for nothing. I was stuck with Con Murphy's tenner. It meant that if Kilkenny lost, I too would be working for my boss for nothing for a month.

The game turned out to be a classic, a heart-palpitating affair which was decided by a last-minute winning point from Terry Leahy which gave Kilkenny the title. I never enjoyed any of it. Visions of losing that bet and its consequences for me kept me in such a state of nerves that the splendour of it all was lost on me. I winced every time Cork scored; I groaned every time Kilkenny missed. When Terry Leahy struck that winning Kilkenny point from 50 yards on the Cusack stand side of the field in the closing minutes, my head was already down between my knees. I just hadn't the nerve to watch him score that all-important winning point to capture Kilkenny's 13th All-Ireland crown. Never

after that did I make or accept a bet on a match. I had learned a very valuable lesson.

Weeks before the historic All-Ireland football final of 1947, GAA secretary general Pádraig Ó Caoimh, in New York, had worked day and night to ensure that everything was in apple pie order for the big day. He knew that a lot was at stake and his reputation as the country's most efficient sporting figure-head was on the line. For one thing, a whole new set of arrangements had to be put in place which were never required for a game in Ireland. A huge reception had to be organised for the Irish party on their arrival, a banquet for 1,500 guests, a New York mayoral reception for the American sporting press, as well as boat and plane reservations for a party of 67, and a wide variety of pre-match publicity events. There had to be radio coverage of the game to Ireland with Michael O'Hehir as commentator. It was going to be a game which O'Hehir would never forget. The venue for the historic occasion was the Polo Grounds at 157th Street and St Nicholas Avenue in the Bronx, which housed many major sporting events including heavyweight fights and was still the home ground of the Giants baseball team. The club would later move to Candlestick Park in San Francisco in 1958 and the Polo Grounds demolished and replaced by an apartment block. But at that time of the year the baseball season was still in progress, and the pitcher's

The 1953 NFL semi-final Dublin team. BACK ROW, LEFT TO RIGHT: *Denis Mahony, Bernie Atkins, Mick Moylan, Jim Crowley, Nicky Maher, Norman Allen, Kevin Heffernan, Tim Mahony.* FRONT ROW, LEFT TO RIGHT: *Tony Young, Cyril Freaney, Tony O'Grady, Sean Scally, Maurice Whelan, Ollie Freaney, Des Ferguson.*

Dublin v Kerry in the Polo Ground, New York, 3 June 1956.

Jim Prior (Faughs), captain of Dublin's senior hurling team, receives the Leinster trophy 1952 from Leinster Council chairman Jack Fitzgerald (Meath).

mound, an area of approximately a square yard raised up some inches from the ground, was still on the pitch. No amount of pleading by the GAA officials succeeded in having it removed.

The weather in New York was 86 degrees and very muggy. On the day before the big game Michael O'Hehir arrived at the venue to check out the broadcasting facilities. The caretaker showed him the broadcasting box, which was also used for baseball games. To Michael's astonishment there was nothing to suggest that the broadcast lines from the international telephone exchange had been installed. The caretaker had no knowledge of a match broadcast either. A very anxious Michael O'Hehir immediately contacted Pádraig Ó

Caoimh. Radio Éireann at that time had never broadcast any event of any kind from America, and being under the aegis of the Department of Posts and Telegraphs and an arm of the civil service, they had to go to the Department of Finance to fund the venture. The story is told that when the radio director at the time, Séamus Ó Braonain, who had won four All-Ireland football medals with Dublin, met the secretary of the Dept of Finance to ask for the money to put in the lines at the American end for the match, he was asked: 'Tell me, does anybody listen to these football matches?' It was decided that Radio Éireann would pay for the cost of the broadcast lines, while the GAA would cover the cost of sending Michael O'Hehir to America and his

Dublin National Football League winners 1953. BACK ROW, LEFT TO RIGHT: *Cyril Freaney, Denis Mahony, Tony O'Grady, Jimmy Lavin, Tony Young, Mark Wilson, Ollie Freaney, S. Farren.* FRONT ROW, LEFT TO RIGHT: *Kevin Heffernan, Jim Crowley, Norman Allen, Mossie Whelan, Nicky Maher, Mick Moylan, Bernie Atkins, Dessie Ferguson, G. O'Toole.*

expenses in New York.

It took the intercession of Mayor Bill O'Dwyer to sort out the broadcasting line problem, when approached to do so by Pádraig Ó Caoimh. It seems that when the GAA general secretary made his eventual comprehensive report to the central council, he told the council members that the American telephone company accepted full responsibility for the broadcasting line cock-up, admitting that the instructions sent on by the London telegraphic authorities were misinterpreted on the American side. However, it wasn't to be the last of the line saga. The lines had been pre-booked to start at 3.30 p.m. and reserved until 5 p.m., which was thought would be adequate to cover the game.

Everything was in order for the big occasion. The heat was stifling (86 degrees) and there was high humidity when the Kerry and Cavan teams paraded around the stadium. 34,941 spectators were in attendance who had paid $153, 877 (then £38,469). Local GAA officials claimed but for the torrential rain the day before, over 54,000 would have been at the match. The game itself was a thriller all the way as the country listened in to Michael O'Hehir's exciting and historic commentary. It amazed everyone how the Kerry and Cavan players measured up to the intense heat. Bottled water was used extensively to keep the players on their feet. Both teams played like men inspired and both were cheered by the huge following. At half-time Cavan led by 2-5 to 2-4.

Cavan still led by a point going into the last quarter with about ten minutes left according to Michael O'Hehir's watch, but he was rocked back in his seat when he saw the stadium clock showing the time at five minutes to five. The pre-match ceremonies, including the introductions of all the dignitaries to the crowd and a special welcome for Mayor O'Dwyer, meant that the preliminaries had gone well over time and the game actually started late.

Michael O'Hehir's commentary was reaching fever pitch as Kerry battled all the way to get on even terms. Realising that the game was not going to end before the 5 o'clock deadline, when the broadcasting line would have the plug pulled, he became frantic and started begging whoever was in charge of the line to allow him five more minutes, and not to pull the plug. Cavan were hanging on desperately by two points scored by Peter Donohoe, who was the prime scorer and was named the 'Babe Ruth' of Gaelic football. O'Hehir was still pleading to be allowed to finish his match commentary with minutes left to play. The wily Mick Higgins, always the big danger in the Cavan attack, kicked two more points to ease the Cavan nerves. Michael O'Hehir kept pleading to leave the line intact, not knowing if he was still being heard back in Ireland.

Leinster final replay 1953, Dublin v Kilkenny. Noel Drumgoole (Dublin), Norman Allen (BEHIND, LEFT) *and Dessie Ferguson* (RIGHT).

Cavan were hanging on, fighting off tremendous pressure from Kerry. There was one last gasp from Kerry. Substitute Tim Brosnan charged towards the Cavan defensive wall, broke through, and with only the Cavan goalie Vincent Gannon to beat, crashed the ball against the crossbar. The ball was cleared to safety by Simon Deignan. That was it. Cavan were All-Ireland champions again after a 12-year gap, winning 2-11 to 2-7 in a game brilliantly handled by referee Martin O'Neill (Wexford).

Michael O'Hehir's pleas not to pull the plug succeeded. He or she down the line answered his prayer. He was given six extra minutes to finish his commentary. It was the last occasion in which an All-Ireland football final was played outside the country. But there was genuine appreciation expressed in many quarters on the decision to take the match to the US, despite a lot of opposition at home. The final certainly revived interest in the national games in the States, and out of the handsome £10,200 profit, the New York board received a grant of £2,000 towards the promotion of the games in the United States.

Torrential rain had fallen all day on Saturday, which kept the attendance down. Even so, the association was pleased with the great work of Pádraig Ó Caoimh, Pádraig McNamee and the New York

The Dublin team who played Mayo in the All-Ireland semi-final in 1955. BACK ROW, LEFT TO RIGHT: *Ollie Freaney, Paddy Flaherty, Dean McGuinness, Mark Wilson, Jim Crowley, Mick Moylan, Jim Lavin.* FRONT ROW, LEFT TO RIGHT: *Maurice Whelan, Nicky Maher, Denis Mahony, Cathal O'Leary, Johnny Boyle, Kevin Heffernan, Dessie Ferguson, Pádraig Haughey.*

The Dublin team who played Kerry in the 1955 All-Ireland football final on 25 September in Croke Park. BACK ROW, LEFT TO RIGHT: *Ollie Freaney, Paddy Flaherty, Sean McGuinness, Jim Crowley, Mick Moylan, Jim Lavin, Terry Jennings, Joe Brennan, Kevin Heffernan, Jimmy Grey.* FRONT ROW, LEFT TO RIGHT: *Johnny Boyle, Cyril Freaney, Cathal O'Leary, Norman Allen, Maurice Whelan, Nicky Maher, Denis Mahony, Dean Manning, Billy Monks, Pádraig Haughey, Des Ferguson.*

officials led by John Kerry O'Donnell, one of the original proposers of the idea. The GAA had to pay all the expenses incurred by Radio Éireann, since the station had made no provision in its estimates for such a costly broadcast. But it wasn't the last time that a crux would arise concerning the playing of a major GAA game in New York.

In 1951 the National League final between Meath and New York was played in Gaelic Park. Radio Éireann agreed to pay the circuit cost, about £300, but the GAA would not pay to send Michael O'Hehir as they had done in 1947. In order to have coverage of the match, Radio Éireann agreed to allow a local commentator, John 'Lefty' Devine to do the broadcast. Listeners in Ireland were very unhappy about Lefty's style of commentary. He got very much taken with the great Meath full back, Paddy O'Brien, whom he called 'Big Hands' O'Brien, and he also had a few quaint names for other Meath players. Frankie Byrne, though small in stature perhaps, was nevertheless a brilliant marksman. He scored six of his side's ten points. He got the tag 'the pocket dynamo'. There were long recriminations as to whether the fault of employing a local commentator lay with Radio Éireann or with the GAA. Ironically, Lefty was a big hit in many quarters here in Ireland, and the genial

Action from the 1955 All-Ireland football final in Croke Park when Dublin met Kerry in an epic encounter.

A section of the crowd at the 1955 Dublin v Kerry All-Ireland football final in Croke Park.

'Big Hands' O'Brien still enjoys a mention of it.

The year 1948 was significant not alone on the sporting front but also on the political scene. A new political party, Clann na Poblachta, emerged, taking up the mantle of republicanism and headed by Seán MacBride. Erskine Childers, Seán MacEntee's parliamentary secretary, greatly alarmed by the rise of Clann na Poblachta, had noted the growing disillusionment with Fianna Fáil even among its own supporters by 1947. He conveyed his fears in a memorandum to MacEntee, stressing the worries he felt of an electoral meltdown, a fate which had befallen Winston Churchill and his Conservative Party in 1945 when the war ended.

In the 1948 election, Fianna Fáil, after 16 years in office, were replaced by a Coalition government headed by John A. Costello of Fine Gael, a former attorney-general, Clann na Poblachta, Labour, and farming and independent representatives. The outcome of the election caused no hand-wringing at GAA level. It was clear

The Dublin team photo before the All-Ireland final against Derry at Croke Park in 1958. BACK ROW, LEFT TO RIGHT: *Denis Mahony, Cathal O'Leary, Paddy O'Flaherty, John Timmons, Lar Foley, Johnny Joyce, Jim Crowley, Mark Wilson, Seán 'Yank' Murray, Brendan Morris, Tony Gillen, Dermot McCann, Paddy Downey, Joey Brennan, Joe Timmons.* FRONT ROW, LEFT TO RIGHT: *Peter O'Reilly* (TRAINER), *Ollie Freaney, Johnny Boyle, Kevin Heffernan* (CAPTAIN), *Paddy Farnan, Mossie Whelan, Christy Leaney, Paddy 'Jock' Haughey, Des Ferguson, Brendan Quinn.*

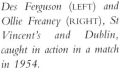

Des Ferguson (LEFT) *and Ollie Freaney* (RIGHT)*, St Vincent's and Dublin, caught in action in a match in 1954.*

that several Gaels had close links with Clann na Poblachta and some had been among the Clann members interned during the war years.

The inter-party government (1948 to 1951) would appear to have been as ideologically committed to protectionism and the promotion of agriculture as the most ardent Fianna Fáil minister. Thanks to the infusion of a small grant from Marshall Aid, the government tried to boost a flagging economy by investing in agriculture, but this investment did not pay dividends as agricultural commodities faced stagnant prices because of the British 'cheap food' policy. It was also stressed within the cabinet that it was next to useless at providing extra employment. When the inter-party government fell in 1951, Fianna Fáil returned to power with Seán MacEntee as Minister for Finance and he began to pursue a vigorous deflationary policy in the 1951–54 term. Muintir na Tire, a non-political movement that exerted much influence on Irish rural life, was warmly supported by the GAA. Founded by Canon Hayes of Bansha in 1937, it made a significant contribution to the improvement of rural life in Ireland. Canon Hayes was a staunch GAA follower and on one occasion attended a hurling match in Buenos Aires. He had been at the

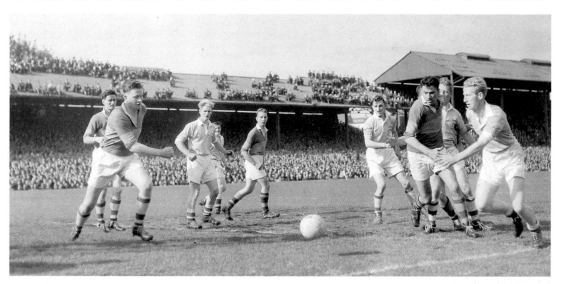

Ned Roche of Kerry goes for a loose ball in the All-Ireland football final against Dublin at Croke Park on 25 September 1955.

The toss-up before the All-Ireland final at Croke Park in 1958. FROM LEFT TO RIGHT: *Kevin Heffernan (Dublin), George Hughes, Simon Deignan (*REFEREE*), Jim McKeever (Derry).*

Supporters pack the stands for the 1958 All-Ireland football final.

Eucharistic Congress in the Argentinian capital and was invited to throw in the ball at a hurling match in Gaelic Park. Afterwards he said: 'A better game of hurling I never saw at home. There was a great spirit of sportsmanship combined with enthusiasm. When the game was over the exiles gathered for a ceili in a beautiful hall which stood in the grounds. Far away in the land of the Southern Cross, these Gaels were carrying on the grand traditions of our native games.'

In 1948 Dublin qualified for the All-Ireland senior hurling final against Waterford and hopes were high that we might repeat the great victory of the 1938 team, which had defeated Waterford to capture the county's sixth All-Ireland crown. Alas it was not to be. A better-drilled Deise side were in no mood for a second defeat at the hands of the city men in an All-Ireland decider. Dublin had no excuses to offer as we went down by 6-7 to 4-2. But I savoured every moment of that final. Playing in an All-Ireland final gives one a sense of participation that no other occasion engenders. Only those who have been part of it can appreciate its humbling effect in defeat or its uplifting grandeur in victory. One way or another, it is an occasion to be savoured, and that 1948 final will always be something special for me because I was part of it.

Ireland was still counting the cost of the effects of World War II, with industrial production down by 30 per cent, and bad weather had hit agricultural production very badly. Unemployment figures stood at 63,500 men and 8,000 women, and the number of people emigrating continued to rise, reaching a total of 40,000 for the year 1948. There was still a lot of food rationing, coal supplies were limited and petrol was still scarce. However, on the credit side some foodstuffs remained plentiful and supplies of bacon, dairy products, canned meats and baby food were soon being exported to Britain.

Sweden and Switzerland, both neutral countries, recovered far more quickly after the war than Ireland did. The economies of both those countries had stronger bases, while their industries had been strengthened by the military expenditure of the warring nations. However, the war did bring about changes in Ireland. When the Fianna Fáil government returned to power after the fall of the coalition government in 1951, Seán Lemass became Minister for Industry and Commerce. Éamon de Valera harboured plans to create suburbs around Dublin as they had done when in power in 1933. The health services were developed and improved greatly. Ireland was facing a new world which was emerging and the dearth of fuel supplies led to the development of

Action from the Dublin v Derry All-Ireland final of 1958. Dublin players: Paddy Farnan (13) with his back to the camera and Johnny Joyce (14) jumping for the ball amongst the Derry players.

The teams parade on to the pitch before the Dublin v Derry All-Ireland final of 1958. Derry captain Jim McKeever leads the Derry team.

Bord na Mona, which was highly successful in industrialising the recovery of peat for fuel. Ireland began picking itself up and national pride was once more restored as our industries began to flourish, making the point once and for all that this was a country determined to stand on its own two feet. Naturally, we still depended on Britain for most of our exports, as we had done prior to the war, but our image of a self-sustaining country was irrevocably altered. It can be stressed that the GAA expanded its activities in the post-war period, helped by the dominance of the Fianna Fáil Party when in government.

That was due to the fact that Fianna Fáil has been unequivocal in its support of our national games and native culture. In addition, from its foundation Fianna Fáil has drawn much of its support from rural Ireland, which the GAA has also done since its foundation in 1884, so naturally there has inevitably been a substantial overlap of membership between the two organisations. On the opposite side of the coin, the second largest party, Fine Gael, while having prominent members either involved in GAA activities or openly supporting the GAA, has from the mid-1930s appeared less enthusiastic in its commitment to the aims and ideals of the GAA.

It is said that part of the reason for this is probably that the Fine Gael Party draws its support mainly from those sections of the urban community whose favourite sports are rugby and soccer. At the same time, the lukewarm attitude of the founder and leader of Fianna Fáil, Éamon de Valera, to Gaelic games was for many members of the GAA a source of disappointment. De Valera had through his long association with Blackrock College in Dublin developed an early and lasting attachment to rugby football. This partiality for what has remained essentially an English and bourgeois brand of football was at variance with the strong nationalist outlook of Fianna Fáil.

Pádraig Ó Caoimh (in his report to the 1952 Congress) stated:

The tragedy of our time is that so many are going away — their fine youth and strength going to the service of other countries. If our association can but convince these young people that Ireland has first claim on their loyalty and that here at home their true welfare and happiness lie, it will not have been founded in vain.

The three men with whom the founding of the GAA has been traditionally associated had much in common, but it may be said that Cusack represented the Gaelic ideal, Davin the athletic and Archbishop Croke the disciplinary ideal. It was this triple combination that gave the organisation its vitality, its durability and its dynamic influence in the social

View of the Hogan stand before the 1958 All-Ireland final.

life of this country . . . its place in Irish life secure, for it is the magnet that draws into its ranks the best elements of our nationally minded people.

In 1952/53 the Dublin footballers captured the sporting headlines by achieving a once-in-a-lifetime feat which commanded the newspaper headlines for some time after the event. When the National Leagues were launched in the 1925/26 period, the football series was played in groups and it wasn't until much later that the format was changed to the present system. There was another extension to the league in the 1960s when the home league winners travelled to the US and played for the league title against New York. That was all changed again in the 1970s.

Dublin had chalked up 15 All-Ireland senior football titles before the county succeeded in capturing their first National League crown and that came in a most astonishing way. The St Vincent's club on the northside of the city became the kingpins of football. They won seven county football championship titles (1949 –55). In the National League final of 1952/53 the Dublin team which played Cavan, the reigning All-Ireland champions, was comprised of 14 St Vincent's players. The exception was goalkeeper Tony O'Grady of the Air Corps. Not alone did they capture the county's first league title, but they won it

on merit by 4-6 to 0-9. Oliver Freaney figured prominently in the Dublin attack along with his brother Cyril, Kevin Heffernan and Dessie Ferguson.

Cyril made an interesting observation to me.

That St Vincent's team was virtually unchanged in personnel for a couple of seasons in league and championship. We were so well drilled in team work that we knew precisely what every player would do with the ball when he gained possession. Left-side defenders would clear to the opposite wing, and the forward anticipated that clearance. The same tactic applied to the right-side defenders, who crossed the ball to the left side to the forward running on to it. We were so well versed in tactical running and passing that our preparations for big games at that time came naturally to us. There was no basketball-type passing as we see in the game played today. We kicked the ball in our passing movements and played directly for our scores. More important still, we had that insatiable appetite to win matches so much that we feared no one.

There was another factor which helped that unique team to achieve football glory. The trainer was none other than Peter O'Reilly (St Mary's, Saggart) who was one of the stars of the 1942 winning All-

Ireland team. Peter's father was Sergeant Michael O'Reilly who had trained Kildare to win the All-Ireland title in 1929 and went on to train Cavan in some of their glorious years in the 1930s. But that 1952/53 National League Dublin success was something special and it will always be one of the most remembered achievements of that great St Vincent's team, who certainly carved the club's name with pride in football lore. The history-making Dublin team lined out as follows: Tony O'Grady (Air Corps), Denis Mahony, Mick Moylan, Mark Wilson, Jimmy Lavin, Norman Allen, Nicky Maher, Maurice Whelan, Jim Crowley, Dessie Ferguson, Ollie Freaney, Cyril Freaney, Bernie Atkins, Tony Young, Kevin Heffernan (all St Vincent's).

Following their 1952/3 league success, Dublin were looking forward to their first All-Ireland appearance since 1942, when they were again pitted against their great rivals, Kerry, in 1955. It was a final in which the media hype focused more on the 'Dublin machine' to outwit and outplay the Kerry 'traditionalists'. Dublin's style of football had gripped the imagination of neutral followers. Their fast attacking forwards had put paid to all kinds of defensive cover in their path to the final. Kerry, who were unimpressive when disposing of Cavan in the semi-final replay, faced a gigantic task, it was stressed, against this formidable city combination. The signs were false. The attendance of 87,102 was boosted to over 90,000 when a gate was broken down and thousands more flocked in. There had been better footballing occasions perhaps, but nothing like the awesome atmosphere which prevailed in the closing ten minutes as Dublin fought for the equalising goal after Ollie Freaney had scored a goal from a 14 yard free. Dublin camped in the Kerry half, but there to thwart their every effort was the lion-hearted Jerome O'Shea, the Kerry corner back. He made two soaring saves under the Kerry crossbar to deny the gallant Dubs each time. As matters subsequently proved, the injuries suffered by Marcus Wilson, Jim McGuinness and Norman Allen in the semi-final replay against Mayo proved too much of a handicap.

McGuinness was given pain killers to ease a knee injury received in training and lined out against Kerry but was forced to retire early in the game. 'Snitchie' Ferguson summed up the general feeling in the Dublin camp when he said to me after the match: 'We let the hype get to us. We lacked a wise old head in our ranks who could have warned us from experience that there is nothing soft in an All-Ireland final, especially against a Kerry team. But the loss of Marcus Wilson and Jim McGuinness, our two best midfielders, and Norman Allen, cost us dearly on the day.'

Many major decisions were having far-reaching effects on the GAA throughout the country in the 1950s. One of the biggest events was the opening of Casement Park, Belfast, a lasting symbol of national unity. Relays of runners from the NACA brought urns of soil from Thurles and Croke Park to be added to the Casement pitch. Pádraig Ó Caoimh presented his 25th annual report to Congress. There were 2,436 affiliated clubs, and income for the previous year was more than £50,000. The report of a subcommittee appointed to consider the full-time training of teams was presented. The committee concluded that such a

Dublin captain Kevin Heffernan jumps for the ball at the throw-in of the 1958 All-Ireland football final.

Dublin's Johnny Joyce (CENTRE) *out-masters Derry goalkeeper P. Gormley for Dublin's second goal in the 1958 All-Ireland football final. Paddy Farnan (Dublin) is on the left.*

Derry goalmouth action in the 1958 All-Ireland final. FROM LEFT TO RIGHT: *T. Doherty (Derry), H. McGribben (Derry), Johnny Joyce (Dublin), Kevin Heffernan (Dublin), P. McLarnin (Derry), Seán 'Yank' Murray (Dublin).*

procedure infringed their amateur status. In a vote by the delegates, full-time training was defeated by 95 to 56. A request that Galway be allowed to compete in the Leinster and Munster hurling championships in alternate years was also defeated.

1954 was the year of the famed Rackard brothers, Nicky, Bobby and Willie, who became known all over the country. They captured the Leinster senior hurling title at the expense of Dublin but lost out to Cork in the All-Ireland that year. A late Johnny Clifford goal robbed Wexford of victory and gave Christy Ring his eighth All-Ireland medal.

I had the privilege and indeed the honour of bringing Christy Ring to Radio Éireann where I interviewed him on my GAA results programme on that Sunday night. He was very modest about his great achievement of winning eight All-Ireland titles at senior level. When I posed the question if he would now consider retirement, his answer left me in no doubt that he had no intention of hanging up his boots. 'I'll keep playing the game that I love as long as the good God above gives me the strength to do so,' he said to me on the airwaves on that historic occasion. Christy died at 57 years of age in early March 1979.

The GAA launched a new series following agreement with the New York GAA board and Central Council. Cork hurlers and Mayo footballers travelled to New York for the inauguration of the St Brendan cup competition in which Cork won the hurling and Mayo lost to the New York footballers. The 1955 GAA Congress was a two-day meeting in which approval was given, as a temporary measure, to a recommendation that university students be allowed to play for college and home clubs; this was later made permanent. It was also agreed to limit the number of substitutes in a game to three and introduce a 'no stoppage' rule to ensure continuous play. The popularity of Gaelic games during the 1950s was reflected in the fact that attendance records were broken on the occasion of major competitions. Twice in that decade, in 1953 and 1959, the attendance record for the football final was smashed; on two occasions, 1954 and 1956, the hurling final was attended by over 83,000 spectators. The 1955 All-Ireland football final between Kerry and Dublin drew a record crowd of 87,102. The installation of seats under the Cusack stand reduced the capacity of the ground, but the same two counties set up a record figure of 73,588 for their All-Ireland final meeting in 1976.

In 1955, famed Wexford had the consolation of taking the All-Ireland senior hurling title when they defeated Galway to capture a crown last won in 1910. The following year, Wexford crowned a great period in their magnificent hurling history when they made ample amends for their 1954 defeat at the hands of Cork. Watched by 83,300, they beat the Leesiders by a clear six-point margin. The Rackard brothers, Nick O'Donnell, Jim English, the Morrisseys, Ned Wheeler, Podge Kehoe and Tim Flood had entered the ranks of the greats. It can be truly stated that Wexford were the team which brought back all the colour, glamour and excitement to the game of hurling which hasn't been matched since by the purple and gold brigade. The Wexford men of the 1950s have left a legacy of which the county can feel proud and for all to aspire to in the 'model county'.

Dublin's defeat by Kerry in the 1955 All-Ireland football final at least indicated the possibility that the basis for an All-Ireland success had been established. Three years later Dublin were back in the race. It was perhaps fitting that the men who had dominated Dublin football teams during the 1950s were at last rewarded when the city men were pitted against Derry in the 1958 All-Ireland senior football final. Captained by Kevin Heffernan, the Dublin men were a vastly experienced team who were not going to repeat the errors of the 1955 defeat by Kerry. Once again ten St Vincent's players dominated the selection, nine of whom played, and Maurice Whelan added significantly to the outcome when he was brought in as a sub for the injured Seán Murray. It was ranked as the greatest Dublin team of the middle and late 1950s.

In five years they won the Leinster title three times, reached two All-Ireland finals and won once (1958), and won three National League titles. The big double was brought off in 1958 and it was the firm belief then, which still lingers, that the double would have been achieved earlier in 1956 but for being committed to play Kerry in New York. The semi-final against Cork was drawn and before the replay the Dublin players had had their travel vaccinations. Marcus Wilson and Mick Moylan reacted so badly that they missed the replay, and with most of the team, notably Denis Mahony, Kevin Heffernan and Ollie Freaney clearly affected, they lost to Cork by 1-16 to 1-9. Further, on their return from New York they lost to Wexford in the first round of the championship, their only defeat in Leinster in five years, apart from that by Louth in the 1957 final.

But all was forgotten in the glory year of 1958. The striplings of the year before were now at their zenith, and a great football team had taken shape. In the final, before an attendance of 73,371, their opponents, Derry, who had shocked the Gaelic world by beating Kerry in the semi-final, could make no real impression on Dublin, who in a half-hour of missed chances at both ends led 0-8 to 0-4 at half-time. Derry to their credit hit top form in the last quarter, and inspired by that great midfielder, Jim McKeever, they battled back to get on terms. Dublin made

Derry captain Jim McKeever shoots for goal in the 1958 All-Ireland football final. Dublin players Mark Wilson (LEFT) *and Joe Timmons* (CENTRE) *look on.*

a match-winning stroke by bringing on Maurice Whelan to corner back, and Lar Foley was switched to midfield on McKeever. That halted the Derry resurgence. Dublin regained the initiative and a last-minute goal from the powerful Johnny Joyce saw Dublin home to victory.

Incidentally, for his play against Kerry and Dublin, Jim McKeever became the first winner of the Texaco trophy as Gaelic Footballer of the Year in 1958. Former defender Denis Mahony was the delighted Dublin county board chairman who watched the team capture the county's 16th All-Ireland title. Another Dublin chairman many years later, former star hurling goalkeeper Jimmy Gray, was to make a decision which created an even greater piece of football history.

Dublin's All-Ireland success in 1958 heralded their first senior title win in 16 years. Kevin Heffernan became the first St

Crowd scene at the 1958 All-Ireland football final, Dublin v Kerry.

Vincent's player to captain a Dublin All-Ireland senior winning side. In the semi-final that year Dublin defeated Galway in a thriller. The winning point came from an Ollie Freaney close free. There was another twist to that game and it centred on one player, Johnny Joyce, whose two brilliant goals at vital stages in the second half set Dublin on the road to victory.

Dublin selector Cyril Freaney vividly recalled what might have been a disastrous blunder and his part in it. Late in the second half the Dublin selectors conferred and decided to replace Johnny. Cyril was deputised to carry out the instructions. He proceeded to make his way behind the Railway goal and endeavoured to attract Johnny Joyce's attention at full forward. But due to the incessant crowd noise Johnny couldn't hear him. As Cyril moved closer to the pitch from behind the Galway goal area, a high speculative lob was sent towards the Galway square. Suddenly, in a blinding flash of brilliance, Joyce collected the high ball, swerved around two defenders and crashed the ball to the Galway net. Cyril recalled ducking as he thought the ball would come through the netting. The incident left Cyril in a quandary as to what to do next. However, his mind was quickly made up for him, as in the next moment Johnny proceeded to repeat the performance with an equally superb goal. That was Cyril's answer, forcing him to return sheepishly

but elated to join his colleagues on the selectors' bench. It was a day which provided the Foley family with a unique honour. Lar won a first All-Ireland senior medal that year, while younger brother Des captained the Dublin minors in their All-Ireland final victory over Mayo.

It was a day that set up another unique record for the St Vincent's club. Both victories ensured that the greatest number of All-Ireland medals ever won by any one club on the same day was established. In addition to the 12 senior players, the club supplied six members to the winning All-Ireland minor panel: Des Foley (capt), Noel Fox, Mick Kissane, Jack Gilroy, and Simon and Paddy Behan. For the record, the senior panel were: Kevin Heffernan (capt), Jim Crowley, Marcus Wilson, Maurice Whelan, Lar Foley, Cathal O'Leary, Des Ferguson, Oliver Freaney, Pádraig Haughey, Paddy Farnan, Johnny Joyce and Christy 'Buster' Leaney. They had the assistance of the mighty 'outsiders', the Timmons brothers (Joe and John), Johnny Boyle, Seán 'Yank' Murray and Paddy Flaherty (goalkeeper).

Pádraig Ó Caoimh's wisdom was clearly demonstrated in his reports to Congress, and that trend is currently carried on by the present ard stiurthoir, Liam Ó Maolmhichil. Many excellent suggestions covering improvements to the structure of the association and towards streamlining the playing end of matters dealing with our games were not always picked up by the respective provincial or county bodies. Many times Ó Caoimh stressed that the ultimate aim of the GAA, as far as grounds were concerned, was a playing field for every club, a first-class ground for every county and at least one fully equipped stadium in each province. Certainly, looking back over the years since that suggestion was first mooted, it is fair to say that the GAA never lost sight of Ó Caoimh's aspiration. Today the GAA possesses the finest stadium in Europe at Croke Park. It is the envy of every sporting organisation in this country and beyond. And the GAA must be congratulated for their commitment, courage, initiative and foresight in providing this wonderful amenity which attracted world-wide attention when the Special Olympics were staged there in 2002. At Easter 1958, Ó Caoimh stated in his report to Congress that 10,000 booklets containing the Gaelic version of all terms used in games had been circulated free of charge to schools and clubs. In addition, a total of £21,627 had been given to the Gaelic League and 350 scholarships were being provided out of GAA funds.

The 75th anniversary of the founding of the GAA (1959) saw New York hurlers defeat Wexford in the St Brendan cup at Croke Park, an event much savoured by New York and Wexford-born Mick Morrissey, who was a tower of strength in the New York defence. The New York footballers made a gallant bid to topple the reigning All-Ireland champions, Dublin, but failed by a two-point margin. Queen's University brought the Sigerson inter-varsity cup to Belfast for the first time. Their hurlers had made the headlines five years earlier by winning the Fitzgibbon cup. Galway hurlers caused a major surprise when they defeated Wexford in the Oireachtas cup final.

On 7 June the GAA proudly opened the new 16,000 capacity Hogan stand, named after Michael Hogan, the Tipperary footballer shot by British forces on 'Bloody Sunday', 1920. The occasion was marked by the Railway cup hurling final which failed to come up to expectations. Munster easily beat an all-Galway Connacht team. Once again the brilliance of Christy Ring made the occasion memorable. Many years later, writing in *Spirit of the Glen*, Christy said: 'My days are over. Let no one say the best hurlers belong to the past. They are with us now and better yet to come.' He certainly was the best in my book. I rate Christy the best hurler I have ever seen, having played against him.

3

Into the Sixties

I remember watching Dublin win their last All-Ireland senior hurling title away back in 1938. The team contained 14 non-natives, with only one Dublin-born player in Jim Byrne from my own club, Eoghan Ruadh. It must be said that the non-native composition in 1938 were hurlers of great repute and represented the best playing in Dublin competitions at the time. They fully deserved their win over a gallant Waterford team, who were to extract full retribution when they beat Dublin ten years later. Dublin's previous senior hurling All-Ireland victory was in 1927. Dublin lost again to Cork in the 1952 All-Ireland final. A motion submitted in 1947 by Gerry O'Connor from the Eoghan Ruadh club to the county board asked that the Dublin hurling team be confined to native-born players and non-natives who played Dublin club hurling from minor grade. The motion was passed by 17 votes to 3. This decision was not implemented until the early 1950s, following the success of the St Vincent's-dominated Dublin football team. I played on the Dublin hurling and football teams on the schoolboys Dublin-Belfast inter-city competitions. That subsequently led to the selection of an all-Dublin senior hurling team to play Antrim, chosen by Gerry O'Connor (Eoghan Ruadh) and

The 1963 All-Ireland football final Dublin team. BACK ROW, LEFT TO RIGHT: *John Timmons, Bill Casey, Mick Kissane, Leo Hickey, Lar Foley, Simon Behan, Pascal Flynn, Brendan Quinn* (TRAINER). FRONT ROW, LEFT TO RIGHT: *Des McKane, Noel Fox, Paddy Holden, Mickey Whelan, Des Foley* (CAPTAIN), *Gerry Davey, Brian McDonald, Des Ferguson.*

Andy Hanratty (St Vincent's). That game fell through because of torrential rain which flooded the Corrigan Park pitch. The team nevertheless had a very enjoyable weekend in Belfast.

After a lapse of nine years, Dublin qualified for the 1961 All-Ireland senior hurling final against the favourites, Tipperary. The team contained 13 native-born players. Paddy Croke, who played minor hurling in Dublin but who was born in Tipperary, and Dessie 'Snitchie' Ferguson, born in County Down but raised in north Dublin, completed the team. This was to be a watershed for Dublin hurling, a summit which had to be attained. Their 7-5 to 4-8 victory over Wexford in the Leinster final had captured

the imagination of the Dublin public and indeed neutral followers as well. The spotlight had always been on the footballers, but now the hurlers had grabbed centre stage. The cherished wish was for a Dublin hurling success to bridge a gap of 77 years and to grab a mead of glory, which up till then had been the preserve of the footballers. The challenge was enormous. They were facing a county which had annexed 17 All-Ireland crowns and who were strong favourites to make it 18.

There were three sets of brothers on the Dublin side. The Foley brothers, Lar and Des, the Fergusons, Dessie and Liam, and the Boothmans, Achill and Bernie. Tipperary's line-out contained some of

Mickey Whelan, manager of St Vincent's, at the Dublin senior football semi-final in October 2005. St Vincent's played Kilmacud Crokes at Parnell Park.

Action photo of the 1961 All-Ireland senior hurling final, Tipperary v Dublin, featuring Dublin players Lar Foley (4) and Noel Drumgoole (3).

the county's legendary figures: John Doyle, Donie Nealon, Tony Wall, Liam Devaney, Jimmy Doyle, Mick Maher and Kieran Carey, to mention some. Tipperary were to capture the honours of the day with a 0-16 to 1-12 scoreline.

There were two specific incidents which ultimately changed the whole complexion of that epic final. The position at half-time was not as clear-cut as the scoreline would suggest. Tipperary led 0-10 to 0-6. Dublin hadn't got into their stride and looked somewhat jittery if not overawed by the occasion. But the attendance of 67,866 never visualised what was awaiting them on the change of ends.

John D. Hickey, writing in the *Irish Independent* the following morning described it as erupting with 'volcanic fury, the memory of which will be treasured by all who watched the combat . . . rarely, if ever, can a final which provided insipid fare in the opening 30 minutes, have furnished such a battle royal in the second period.'

Within less than seven minutes of the resumption Dublin had wiped out Tipperary's lead with a brilliant Billy Jackson goal and a well-taken Achill Boothman point. Larry Shannon shot over a point with a goal there for the taking. Dublin were suddenly in the driving seat and rattled over two more points to lead by a point at the end of the three-quarter stage. An incident then occurred which changed the entire course of the match. Dessie Ferguson was the victim of a wild pull from substitute Tom Ryan (Tipperary) and Lar Foley got involved with Ryan in a mêlée which followed, leaving referee Gerry Fitzgerald (Limerick) with no option but to sideline both players.

Shrewd Tipperary selector Paddy Leahy became apprehensive about the sudden change in the match tempo. Dublin were beginning to get a grip and action was quickly needed. At that stage Tipperary were hanging on desperately to a one-point lead with eight minutes remaining. Leahy made his move and switched Liam Devaney from centre forward to centre back. Devaney had been the central figure in their attack in the first half and had created many scoring chances, put to good use by Jimmy Doyle, Donie Nealon and Matt O'Gara. Dublin stormed the Tipperary goal in the closing stages, but over-anxiety led to a couple of goal-scoring chances being badly missed. The dominance of Devaney in the pivotal role in defence proved Tipperary's master stroke after Tony Wall had retired injured. Devaney, with a masterful display, really broke the hearts of a gallant Dublin attack with an authoritative display for Tipperary in his new role in the rearguard. While Dublin had every reason to bemoan several great goaling chances during the game, I would pinpoint the failure of the Dublin team mentors to make a couple of required positional switches at a crucial stage of the match. Larry Shannon would have played a more vital role as Des Foley's partner at midfield in curbing the power of Matt O'Gara and Theo English. Mick Bohan, who played his club hurling at centre forward, should have been moved there in the second period. I made this point in my *Evening Press* column in the match report.

Jimmy Gray, who had a magnificent game in the Dublin goal, kept a clean sheet against one of the best attacking units at the time. He told me: 'I only had four or five shots to deal with over the hour. We didn't get the luck either on a few occasions which could have turned the game for us. Tipperary were awarded a Matt O'Gara point which, as I saw it, was well wide, but it was allowed. Des Ferguson was penalised for picking up a rolling ball while similar pick-ups by Tipperary went unpunished. It was heartbreaking for Dublin to lose that final. It was perhaps the best display ever given by a Dublin team since the 1938 win over Waterford.' Had Dublin won that All-Ireland title, there is little doubt in my mind that it could have become the launching pad that would have made the hurling Dubs household names for many years afterwards. More importantly, an All-Ireland victory in 1961 for a 'native' team

Pádraig Ó Caoimh (general secretary) addressing the 1958 Annual Congress. Seán Ó Síocháin (assistant secretary) is on the left and Dr J.J. Stuart (GAA president) is on the right.

over Tipperary would have inspired the youth in the capital city to heights never before reached in quest of hurling's 'Holy Grail', the Liam McCarthy cup. Sadly, it was not to be. No Dublin team has since emerged to recapture the brief greatness of the 1961 men's bid for glory. And Dublin have since slipped down the ladder into the background and inexorably no longer pose any threat to the major hurling forces.

To lose an All-Ireland senior hurling final by a single point was heart-breaking enough, but when it involved a native Dublin side the pain was even greater. Had Dublin won in 1961, hurling in the capital city would have been revived, whereas that win for Tipperary simply gave them a statistical boost with an 18th crown. The future of Dublin hurling is very much in the news at present, but it must be remembered that back in 1973 football in the capital city was in the doldrums. A remedy was found through the foresight of the then Dublin board chairman Jimmy Gray. More about him anon.

There is no reason why hurling in Dublin cannot be restored if the means, manpower and finance, which has now been provided, are put to proper use. It happened for the footballers. Why not in hurling? The Schools Primary Leagues followed after the setting up of that body in 1928. The leagues saw the birth of Dublin city hurling and football inter-schools competitions, which laid the

foundation stone for Dublin's rising stars in later years. Ironically, a newspaper comment following a Dublin junior board convention in 1928 read: 'A preposterous motion to confine Dublin teams to natives of the Metropolis was proposed at the Convention on Saturday last. Fancy a Dublin native hurling team!' The Dublin Primary Schools committee is still hale and hearty, turning out countless boys and girls to play the games. Tributes have always been paid to the schools leagues over the years for their work on behalf of the GAA in the capital city, and deservedly so. Long may they continue the great work.

In deference to the Dublin hurlers, it must be said that the lack of success on their part over the years at top level is now reflected in the poor support they have been accorded, and more is the pity. It has led to a delicate situation wherein the dual player is now more likely to give his allegiance to the football team rather than the hurling side.

Undoubtedly, the 1961 team which last contested an All-Ireland senior hurling final enjoyed the greatest support ever accorded a Dublin team because it was predominately a Dublin native selection. The powerful 1927 side which humbled Cork in the All-Ireland hurling final by 4-8 to 1-3 was drawn from the top hurling counties and was, in effect, given the unkind appellation, a 'League of Nations' selection. It was noticeable, following another defeat in 1961, that the supporters once again turned to the footballers, who appeared a more viable proposition for support at All-Ireland level. Unlike their hurling counterparts, the footballers had at least savoured success at top level and were more likely to do so again.

⁂

During the period 1958 to 1963, the Republic of Ireland became a more open, questioning, self-confident society, and many factors helped produce this satisfactory state of affairs. During the next six years, 1958 to 1964, the country's growth rate shot forward to 4 per cent — a very respectable figure by European standards and better than that achieved by Britain. The sudden injection of wealth manifested itself in different ways. Wages went up; so did social welfare benefits. A new breed of entrepreneurs came to the fore. New office blocks rose in Dublin posing challenges for those who wished to preserve the capital's Georgian architecture. New types of retail outlets, the supermarket and the self-service shop, were opened. The number of cars on the road leapt upwards, so much so that the Republic had to break away from the old easygoing tradition and introduce driving tests for new drivers.

The most potent new influence within the Republic however was, without doubt, television. To some extent its influence began even before the period covered by these reminiscences. From the early 1950s it was possible to pick up signals from the BBC and ITV transmitters in areas near enough to Wales or Northern Ireland. Naturally, this 'free' service or supply developed one of the most characteristic features of the Dublin skyline in that period — the forest of tall aerials erected to pick up distant signals from British transmitters.

But the real impact began with the inauguration of a domestic service, Teilifís Éireann, on 31 December 1961. Teilifís, unlike the British stations, covered the whole of the Republic, and its programmes catered directly for an Irish audience. Teilifís Éireann was soon provoking an examination of established Irish institutions and values on a scale hitherto unknown. The nature of the medium dictated this. It may have taken Teilifís some years to work its way through a full appreciation of the possibilities of the medium, and its greatest impact did not come until the late 1960s, but its influence was growing.

In programmes such as the *Late Late Show* compered by Gay Byrne, there were increasingly frank discussions in public, ranging from the role of the clergy to controversial sexual matters. I worked in the medium right from the start with the setting up of the sports division under Michael O'Hehir. There was great excitement surrounding the launch of television. I was among a group of men who attended a temporary studio in Marian College in Sandymount where Phil Thompson, on loan from the BBC, put us through our paces in front of the camera. It was very evident from that particular lesson that those of us who were experienced in radio sport programmes had a much better grasp of the fundamentals of television broadcasting, in comparison with our colleagues from the newspapers who had no experience of either. When television started I was one of the commentators selected on a freelance basis. I believed that TV match commentaries were very different from those on radio, the prime reason being that

the viewer was seeing the action at the same time as the commentator, so there was very little use in describing the obvious.

I had the rare distinction of being chosen to do the first live commentary on the All-Ireland hurling final between Tipperary and Wexford in 1962, and the All-Ireland football final that year between Roscommon and Kerry. A decision was taken, however, that I would do the commentary in English for the opening quarter and Micheal Ó Muircertaigh would take over and do the next quarter of the game in Irish. It was one of those Irish solutions to an Irish problem. A motion

Galway captain Mick Garrett leads the team in parade before the 1963 All-Ireland final against Dublin.

had been passed at the GAA Congress earlier that year that more Irish should be used in the transmission of Gaelic games on television. There was never any suggestion of doing a bilingual commentary on radio for obvious reasons, one being that it would not have been possible, or tolerated.

The experiment of doing the All-Ireland finals in 1962 bilingually came in for a lot of criticism at the time. It was generally felt that a better purpose would have been served had the game gone out in its entirety in Irish, or alternatively in English, but not a mixture of both. The following year the head of sport, Michael O'Hehir, decided that he would do a simultaneous commentary on the All-Ireland finals on radio and television. Wisely, it wasn't repeated.

Michael O'Hehir and I differed from time to time over the amount of dialogue I was using in my television commentaries. He felt it needed more, on the radio style; I felt I was using a little too much. It remained a bone of contention between us. I still cling to the view that our TV commentators tend to over-indulge themselves when describing action on TV matches and leave little to the imagination of the viewer. The art of television commentary on matches differs greatly now, thankfully, from the early days.

Like most traditional football counties in the GAA, Dublin's rise as a powerful force stemmed from the solid foundation built by the great players of the 1920s, and the then household names, the McDonnells, the Synnotts and the Careys who were all linked with the famous O'Tooles from Seville Place. There were in fact eight Synnott brothers, Tom, Stephen, Jim, Josie, John, Patrick, Leo and Peter. Four of them played on Dublin teams, Stephen, Josie, John and Peter, perhaps the most famous being Stephen, John and Josie. I got to know most of them when I joined the O'Tooles club in the 1940s (I am still a member). Those household names sprang from the docks area of the northside in the parish of St Laurence O'Toole. There were two great clubs in the parish at the time, O'Tooles and St Mary's, and between them they won three All-Irelands in a row for Dublin, 1921, 22 and 23, failing by just one point to Kerry in the memorable 1924 final, and having lost to Tipperary in 1920. With luck it could have been an all-time record of five in a row.

Dublin's surge to the top could be traced back to the All-Ireland junior championship success in 1914. Captained by Paddy Carey (then of Emeralds), the team included many who would subsequently rise to the forefront in the senior grade. After conquering a tough Kilkenny side in the Leinster final — after which Paddy McDonnell and others were nursing bruises for weeks — they beat

Limerick in the final. Thus Paddy McDonnell, the Careys, Steve and Josie Synnott and Kerry-born Paddy Kerins won their first All-Ireland junior medals.

When the McDonnells, the Synnotts and the Careys were young, they made tremendous sacrifices to play the game of their choice. They were stoned and insulted by the advocates of soccer at the Commons on the Church Road. Then a band of Tipperary men — who were employed by the London Midland Scottish Railways (LMS, later British Railways) — formed the Brian Boru's and rowed in with O'Tooles in training. There was no more stone throwing. It must be said that inside ten years Gaelic football had taken such a grip in the parish that there were five senior teams, including St Mary's, St Joseph's and O'Tooles.

O'Tooles travelled the length and breadth of the land in their day. No club was more sought after for challenge games — and no team was as popular. Nearly all the club members were in the Volunteers. Most of them were in E Company, 2nd Battalion, and took their stand in Jacob's factory in 1916. Johnny McDonnell was deported to Knutsford and from there to Frongoch in north Wales. O'Tooles were not just a mere Gaelic team — they were a club and a school for everything Irish and national.

The austerity of wartime and indeed the years after posed major problems for the GAA who, nevertheless, still remained the major attraction in the eyes of the new rising population. The advent of television in the 1960s brought a new challenge as the choice of sports viewing increased and the people began to enjoy greater prosperity. The standard of living rose, workers demanded and got better working conditions, which meant a complete change in the country's lifestyle. But the alarm bells were ringing as attendances at sporting events, even those professed to be keen rivals of the national games, began to fall sharply.

GAA secretary Pádraig Ó Caoimh, who always had his finger on the pulse of the nation, was conscious of the marked social trends which were developing around the country. He had stressed it in his annual reports to Congress and warned of the possible dangers accruing. It was not the competition from other sports to which Ó Caoimh was referring, but to the ever-changing lifestyle of the Irish people, because of the affluence they were enjoying. All sporting bodies, the GAA included, began to suffer from falling attendances in the early 1960s.

There was much concern in GAA circles over the health of Pádraig Ó Caoimh, who had been in indifferent health over a long period. In an attempt to ease his workload, extra staff were appointed, and that included a young Cork schoolteacher, Seán Ó Síocháin, who became Ó Caoimh's assistant secretary. When the GAA supremo died in May

Jackie Gilroy (Dublin) (CENTRE) *chips the ball towards Eamon Breslin (Dublin) as Laois goalie Tom Miller* (RIGHT) *moves across his goal line.*

1964, a few months short of completing 35 years as general secretary, the association lost its greatest figure-head. It must be said that Ó Caoimh was a visionary. Because of his great business acumen he gave the association a place in the life of the country that no other national body could aspire to. In over 50 years as a sports journalist, I never had any problems in my dealings with Pádraig Ó Caoimh. I always found him extremely competent, courteous and most helpful.

In my young days he asked me to announce team changes and important public messages on the occasions of major games at Croke Park, and this I did for many years. It was only in later years that a situation arose where we crossed swords. In 1955, two years after I had taken over the Sunday GAA programme from my father, I received a phone call from the general secretary objecting to the naming of players sent off in matches in my reports on radio. He claimed that it was accepted policy to omit such references 'on air' and he would prefer if I followed those guidelines. The sting came in the tail when he told me that I could always be replaced if I failed to follow that suggestion. I tried to reason with him, pointing out that 40,000 spectators were watching players being sent off at Croke Park, and it didn't make sense not to mention it in my match report if the sending off affected the result.

Eamon Breslin scores his controversial header in a 1964 National Football League game against Laois.

It was all to no avail. He was not for moving on the issue. The veiled threat of being replaced did worry me, so I contacted the then sports officer at Radio Éireann, Philip Greene, and explained my dilemma. The GAA would not put their complaint against me in writing when asked to do so by the station director, Roibeard Ó Farracháin, and that ended the matter. I continued to name players who were sidelined for offences on the field, and it didn't affect my relations later with Pádraig in any way. Nowadays, it is common practice for players sent off for breaking the playing rules to be named by commentators and match reporters.

After Ó Caoimh's death his replacement, assistant Seán Ó Síocháin, was a clear favourite to take over the job. Ó Síocháin, having vast experience of the work, was easily the popular choice for the position. He was popular with the clubs, counties and the public he served. He streamlined the administrative side of matters, but his strength really lay in his ability to perform his duties and still satisfy all the demands that were being made on the association from time to time. He served the GAA very well during his 15 years as chief executive before he retired. I had the privilege of announcing Seán Ó Síocháin's appointment as general secretary from Croke Park on a television programme presented by Michael

O'Hehir on the evening of 28 August 1964. The present occupant of the prestigious position of ard stiurthoir is Longford-born Liam Mulvihill, who is maintaining the high level of administration set by his predecessors.

The 1960s was the decade of the great Down football team who brought a new dimension to Gaelic football with their sophisticated style of power-backed running and skilful play. That decade too saw Tipperary hurling at its brilliant best with star-studded selections capturing the coveted honours with great aplomb.

In the realms of football, 1963 will be remembered as the year Dublin committed wholesale larceny by robbing Galway of the All-Ireland senior football crown. Galway went on the next year to begin an unprecedented three in a row of All-Ireland successes. As history recorded, Dublin had denied Galway a fabulous four in a row sequence of victories when beating the Westerners by 1-9 to 0-10 on 22 September 1963 at Croke Park. It goes without saying that winning an All-Ireland senior football title in any year is a wonderful achievement and beyond one's wildest dreams. But when a totally unfancied side reaches such a pinnacle in sport, it borders on the incredible.

Dublin were still smarting from a humiliating defeat at the hands of Galway in the National League in March that year, but fate was to step in on several fronts to bring about a change of attitude in the Dublin football camp. Brendan Quinn of Parnells was appointed trainer and under his stewardship the air of despondency among the Dublin players began to ease. Renowned All-Ireland winning captain Kevin Heffernan was called in as a Dublin selector for the 1963 championship campaign. To the neutral eye the Dublin team was not viewed as highly as previous teams bidding for All-Ireland glory.

On their way to the 1963 All-Ireland final they were beset by injuries to key players, and yet they progressed by beating Meath 2-6 to 2-5; they beat Kildare 2-7 to 1-5; beat Laois 2-11 to 2-9; and defeated Down in a rather torrid All-Ireland semi-final before 70,072 spectators. The star of that game was undoubtedly Paddy Holden at centre back, flanked by the impressive Des McKane and Mick Kissane. Joe Lennon at midfield was the only Down player to uphold his reputation with a very businesslike performance

Selector Kevin Heffernan was worried about the strength of the Dublin forward division. He felt it needed an experienced figure-head who could hold the ball up and create openings for scores. Heffernan himself could have filled the role admirably. He was still playing great football with his club, St Vincent's, as indeed was his club mate Dessie Ferguson. During a discussion between the players it was agreed that Heffernan should fill the position himself. Then came the bombshell. Heffernan decided that the player most suited to the task of leading the attack was Ferguson. It was a brave decision by Heffernan and it was to pay off handsomely.

Dual performer Ferguson was called into the team for the Leinster semi-final against Kildare three years after he had departed the inter-county scene. He created havoc in the Kildare defence with his roving tactics and superb distribution of the ball, which Simon Behan and Mickey Whelan thrived on by posting brilliant scores. If there was a loud cheer when Ferguson's name was called out in the pre-match announcement, it was nothing like the crescendo of sound that followed when Ferguson, eight minutes from the end, scored the goal that put Dublin into the Leinster final. Also figuring in the attack was Eamon Breslin from Ballyfermot De La Salle, who captured the footballing headlines during a National League match when he headed in a Dublin goal at the Canal end. Anybody can use their feet or hands in quest of scores in Gaelic football, but seldom has a player used his head to better effect than did Dublin's Eamon Breslin. He stunned the spectators on Sunday, 1 November 1964, at Croke Park, when he skilfully headed a goal against Laois to put Dublin on the road to a five-point win. Breslin's 'flying header' was the subject of major controversy all that week.

The lead up to the score was simple enough. Brian McDonald, noted for his ground football during matches, dribbled the ball 10 to 15 yards towards an unmarked Jackie Gilroy on his left. Jackie told me: 'The Laois defence was in complete disarray. I saw Eamon Breslin moving forward and instead of bending down and picking the ball up, I chipped it about head high to Eamon.' Eamon picked up the story. 'The ball was coming towards me and I could see the Laois goalie was off his line, so I just headed the ball to the corner of the net. Had I attempted to catch the ball, the Laois goalie, Tom Miller, would have tackled me, so I just nodded it home, and that was that.' Breslin's goal gave Dublin a lead they never lost.

The newspapers were full of letters claiming the goal should have been disallowed; others saw no penalty in scoring with the head. As an All-Ireland referee, I printed the relevant rule covering the controversy, which stated at the time: 'A goal is scored when the ball is driven or played by either side between the goal posts, and under the cross bar, except when thrown or carried by any of the attacking side' (rule 133, Official Guide). The word 'driven' clearly covers a headed shot, since the only illegal methods specified are 'throwing and carrying'. It is, however, a very rare occurrence which probably accounts for the widespread ignorance of the rule.

I subsequently got a letter to my *Evening Press* column from a Cork reader. He said there had been a Gaelic football club match in Cork, at which an Army team had been engaged. One of the Army players headed the ball over the opposing goal line, whereupon the referee blew his whistle and disallowed the goal, awarding a free to the defending team. He was immediately surrounded by protesting Army players, demanding to know why the goal was disallowed. 'Dangerous play' was the curt reply from the referee, and he restarted the match. It may be presumed that the relevant rule was quoted to the referee later that evening, in the interest of fair play.

For the record, a headed goal is quite within the rules of the game and there is no rule against such a score. Eamon Breslin's historic goal didn't go unnoticed by the media. He was awarded the 'Sports Star' of the week honour by a number of newspapers. Eamon was a brilliant forward in the 60s and figured in all of Dublin's successes. If and when Croke Park is made available to soccer, Eamon Breslin's headed goal will still be the first on the hallowed sod of Croke Park and a place in football history.

The All-Ireland final against Galway was perhaps Dublin's greatest test. Galway of the 1960s were deemed to be the most polished team to emerge from Connacht for years and were very much fancied to regain a title last held in 1956. Galway dominated the game in the first half, but a combination of good defensive work and poor forward finishing saw them leading by only three points. The big danger for Dublin was Galway's big Mattie McDonagh, who was proving a handful for Paddy Holden, and when Holden had to retire with an injury, Dublin's prospects looked decidedly bleak. Not so. The day was saved when Paddy Downey, brought into the action at centre back, played the game of his life.

Another great positional switch by the selectors was to move Mickey Whelan to midfield and rearrange the half backs. The balance was restored. Dublin's winning goal came in the closing minutes. A line ball in by Brian McDonald of Galway appeared to be going wide at the Railway end, but the skilful Simon Behan grabbed the ball and turned towards the Galway goal. As a couple of defenders converged on him, Behan espied Gerry Davey rushing towards the parallelogram and coolly punched the ball over the heads of the Galway backs. Davey's eyes never left the ball as he and Noel Fox sped into the area. Davey's fist met the ball first, giving the Galway goalkeeper Michael Moore no possible chance of stopping it. Dublin, two points ahead now, had to face a stiff onslaught from the Galwaymen as the final minutes ticked away, but the home team held on bravely to win by 1-8 to 0-10. The almost impossible had been achieved and a no-hoper Dublin team, against all the odds, had chalked up the county's 17th All-Ireland crown. It would take Dublin 11 years to reach another senior All-

Ireland final, and fate decreed that the opposition would again be mounted by great rivals, Galway.

The GAA was very conscious of the effect the establishment of Teilifís Éireann would have on its games and its approach was one of extreme caution. Undoubtedly, Teilifís Éireann's use of the All-Ireland finals and semi-finals drove viewing figures sky high, but there was a noticeable drop in attendance figures at the actual matches themselves. But it was to the credit of the GAA that they made the first move towards providing an opening for the national games to be screened when the new medium was launched. The association, as a gesture of goodwill, agreed to accept a nominal sum (ten guineas) for live coverage of the two All-Ireland finals, the two semi-finals and the St Patrick's Day finals. That gesture was a magnanimous decision for a body which controlled the largest sporting organisation in the country. However, the GAA was also concerned about the lack of programmes relating to GAA matters and the general secretary Pádraig Ó Caoimh was constantly seeking a change in that situation. Ó Caoimh's persistence paid off and a special programme (*Gaelic Report*) was launched which this writer presented for some years.

The golden jubilee of the Rising in 1916 was marked by year-long celebrations in 1966 sponsored by the government. Jubilee events were staged throughout the country. Historical pageants were arranged in towns and villages, culminating in one of the most spectacular in Croke Park. 1966 brought a new challenge for the GAA when the World Cup soccer competition was played in England for the first time since it was inaugurated in 1930. Naturally, this event was eagerly looked forward to by soccer enthusiasts and neutrals alike in this country. Teilifís secured permission, at a huge fee, to screen all the main games and used the series to swell their advertising revenue coffers. The Teilifís coverage of the 1966 World Cup competition gave soccer a major boost in this country and it enabled the FAI to establish itself in rural areas, where before they had had no soccer involvement.

Irish politics saw a major change with the retirement of Seán Lemass and the appointment of his successor, Jack Lynch, of Cork All-Ireland fame. He became the first Corkman to lead an Irish government since the death 44 years before of Michael Collins. Lynch was easily the most popular figure in political life at the time, not alone for his past achievements on GAA fields, being a dual winner of six All-Ireland titles, but he was an instant hit with the public and was held in high esteem by all sections of the community. It pleased the GAA very much to have a politician of

Jack Lynch's stature as Taoiseach, a man whose reputation was shaped on the hurling and football fields of this country. He became one of the most able politicians in Dáil Éireann and a fearless Taoiseach.

One of the burning issues at Congress gatherings during the 1960s was the questioning of traditional values by the younger members of the association. In that period there were efforts to abolish the 'ban' (rule 27), which imposed automatic suspension on a member playing, attending or promoting rugby, soccer, hockey or cricket.

A Civil Service football club motion appeared on the clár of the Dublin county convention as far back as 1959 seeking a comprehensive investigation into the rule under the authority of the next congress. Because of a Congress decision of the 1920s to limit discussion of such a rule to every third year, this motion could not get on to a congress agenda until 1962. Four motions, one each from Armagh and Carlow and two from Dublin came before the 1962 Congress. All four motions were defeated by big margins. By the time 1965 came around, those counties who favoured action to remove rule 27 began putting bigger and more favourable cases together for presentation to congress. The most prominent of these anti-ban campaigners was the Dublin Civil Service delegate, Tom Woulfe, who became the Dublin board spokesman for his motion. Woulfe,

Kerry born, kept the movement to abolish the infamous ban alive through his criticism over the years on radio and television and his letters to all the morning and evening newspapers. I sat in the lecture hall in Trinity College, Dublin, listening to Tom Woulfe making his case, very successfully too, for the abolition of the ban against stiff opposition, but he won his case. Congress 1965 produced no change in the association's attitude towards rule 27. The straightforward motion sponsored by Dublin and put by Tom Woulfe and other speakers was again defeated by 230 votes to 52.

Between the congresses of 1965 and 1968 prominent supporters of the ban brought out a booklet written by Brendan McLua entitled 'The Steadfast Rule'. McLua was a member of the Croke Park staff and a talented journalist. He traced the history of the ban principle and rule from the start of the GAA in a carefully researched publication. The mood of those Gaels wanting rule 27 removed from the GAA rule book remained intransigent, as indeed did those favouring its retention. There were indications at the time that the number of counties making strong noises about the actual need for the contentious rule 27 was steadily growing. Nevertheless, Tom Woulfe and his Civil Service club colleague, Eamon Mongey from Mayo, paid visits to counties all over the country seeking support for the rule's deletion.

The 1968 Congress was to prove a high watermark for events relating to the removal of the ban, but that was not realised at the time, even by those who wanted it retained. Motions dealing with the ban appeared on the Congress agenda. Dublin and Galway motions seeking its removal again bit the dust by 220 votes to 88. This time a significant motion from Mayo (similar to those from Limerick and Louth) directing the setting up by the central council of a special committee to make the case for the retention of rule 27, with a directive to publish a report inside three years, was passed, following a well-reasoned and balanced plea from Fr Leo Morahan of the sponsoring board.

The Central Council proceeded to carry out the Mayo proposal by selecting a committee comprised of Tom Loftus (Dublin), Peadar Kearney (Louth), GAA president Séamus Ó Riain (Tipperary), past president Alf Murray (Armagh), Pat Fanning (Waterford, a future president) and Monsignor Hamilton (Clare) who died during the first quarter of the committee's work. He was not replaced. Towards the end of 1970 this committee issued a detailed statement on the ban. It gave a brief run-down on the history of the ban and one-third of the document presented the main arguments for and against rule 27. The main theme of the rest of the report leaned more to the view that the rule should be retained. Finally, the committee's conclusion ended on what might be called a cautiously neutral note by declining to recommend any change to rule 27.

It could be argued that the report in its essence was really favouring the retention of the ban, despite the Mayo motion precluding it from taking an anti-ban line. By the time the report was published, an important move got under way to measure the views of the rank and file of the GAA club members on rule 27. At the 1970 Congress (held in Galway) a Meath motion had been passed unanimously, requiring a special meeting of each club to be called to decide its attitude on the ban rule for the 1971 Congress. Those meetings were held all over the country from late autumn in that year, and by the end of the year it was quite clear that a substantial majority of clubs favoured its removal. This was again the power of the club in action — and the first real indication that the ground swell of club opinion was pointing the way in a matter of great importance for the association. It was a small light at the end of the tunnel. A more dramatic and telling case for the abolition of rule 27 came early in 1971 when 30 counties decided to support any congress move to abolish rule 27. Antrim and Sligo were the only counties to vote for its retention. The position was now very much clarified. After 60 years of its existence the ban was on the brink of extinction.

The death-knell of the ban was most assuredly sounded following the returns

Lar Foley, Dublin senior hurling manager.

from the county conventions, but alarm bells were also ringing in the power halls of the association. The abolition of the ban after 60 years meant a betrayal of what the GAA originally stood for, and some believed it now no longer aspired to the national and cultural aims it had supported for many decades. GAA president Pat Fanning, a staunch pro-ban advocate, was now facing the daunting task of implementing the democratically reached decision of the majority of the members when it came before Congress on 11 April 1971 at Queen's University, Belfast. He drew up proposals to put to Congress simultaneously with the abolition of the ban motion, rule 27, and deferred communicating them beforehand to the pro-ban or the anti-ban groups.

His proposals contained a new charter reasserting the loyalty of the GAA, despite the ending of the ban, to national culture, ensuring the use of the association's resources and property for its own purposes only, and clearly defining for the first time membership of the GAA. He proposed to appoint a small committee of leading members to draft this charter without delay for submission to a special congress to be held inside two months. Fanning, who was a very experienced GAA figure-head, had done his homework well. Fears that an acrimonious debate might result from the discussion on the proposal to abolish the ban never

manifested itself — Fanning saw to that. He addressed the delegates and in carefully measured words he coolly and calmly unfolded his plans in a very dignified way. In one of the most important moments in GAA history, rule 27 'walked the plank and disappeared without trace', a phrase coined by the leading anti-ban spokesman, Tom Woulfe. The hall erupted and Pat Fanning was accorded an unprecedented ovation led by the anti-ban lobby at that Belfast Congress gathering. Within three days Fanning appointed a nine-man committee to draw up the new charter. In May, at a special congress held in Dublin, it took less than two hours to approve all the revised rules contained in the new charter. Under the new rule 1 the basic aim of the GAA is defined as 'the strengthening of the national identity in a 32-county Ireland through the preservation and promotion of Gaelic games and pastimes'. The property of the association is also protected by the same rule. Professionalism of any kind, including full-time training, is banned by the new rule 6. The removal of the ban in 1971 did not lead to an exodus of players to other codes in subsequent years, as was suggested during the debates on the rule.

It can be said that the younger generation played a leading role in changing GAA history in 1971 without a trace of rancour in achieving that end.

4

Heffo

Dublin's glory days had long since vanished in the period between 1963, their last All-Ireland success, and the start of the 1970s. More important still was the fact that the Dublin supporters, who had feasted on the successes of the 1950s and early 60s, had lost their sporting identity. They were no longer prepared to follow a mediocre band of players not prepared to work for success. Dublin board chairman Jimmy Gray was quite the opposite. He was not prepared to allow Dublin football to slip any further into obscurity and started a plan for its recovery. He had a meeting with Kevin Heffernan, the purpose of which was to get the St Vincent's man involved. But Kevin had to turn the invitation down as he had committed himself to managing the 'Vins'. As luck would have it, I happened to ring Jimmy Gray that same day, seeking information on his chat with Kevin. Jimmy explained that Kevin was club-tied. I wrote my piece in the *Evening Press* the following day suggesting that Kevin Heffernan was the only man that could stop the Dublin rot. Whilst I got a tremendous response from my column readers, it also put Kevin under a lot of pressure which I had unwittingly created. The end result was, Kevin phoned Jimmy Gray and told him he would give the Dublin manager's job a go. A delighted Jimmy Gray appointed Donal Colfer (Synge St) and Lorcan Redmond (St Margaret's) as his two selectors. The move ended the old practice of five or six selectors; the burden would now be shouldered by three team officials, with Kevin taking the managerial role.

In the circumstances which Dublin football found itself, it was felt that nothing short of a miracle could restore them to even the first rung of the ladder. But they had not reckoned on Heffernan's capacity, as a football legend himself, to break down barriers.

Kevin, a near neighbour of mine, related a story about a National League football match in Kilkenny in October 1973. When they arrived they couldn't find a parking place for the team coach. Every inch of space was taken up by cars because of the curtain raiser, which turned out to be a local minor championship final. The stand was packed; the atmosphere was electric. They thought the big crowd would add a lot to the senior game. Dublin emerged from the tunnel on to the pitch to find the ground virtually deserted. The huge crowd for the minor game had gone home and only a few handfuls remained. Few supporters followed Dublin teams in those days. Gay O'Driscoll commented: 'It was lucky a

linesman turned up. We could not have supplied one.' Imagine the mind of Kevin Heffernan as the team struggled to beat the lowest rated football team in the country at the time. Come the winter, and Heffernan began putting the pieces together.

Kevin never concealed his optimism about the prospect of moulding a team that he envisaged would open up paths to greater development. I asked him at the time what his priorities were. 'I'll give it to you in two words — communication and physical fitness,' he said. When he took the team in hand at the start of the 1973/74 season, he immediately saw where weaknesses could arise and where changes might be needed to rectify matters. 'It will have to be an exercise in communication. It's always been my view that there's a way that Dublin fellows should play football. Generally, Dublin players are astute players with plenty of speed and good ball control. These are the things I hope to exploit,' he added. Those indeed were the things he put into practice, and from the players he got total commitment.

Dublin's first round win in the Leinster championship at Croke Park against Wexford didn't exactly set the heather blazing. On the way from the match with his wife Mary and Lily Jennings, Kevin said he had to get a good free taker. It was badly needed. Up piped Lily's 10-year-old son Terence: 'Why don't you get Jimmy Keaveney? He's knocking over points every Sunday with the club.' Later that night Jimmy Keaveney's name cropped up again and Kevin eventually got in touch with him and made his pitch. He needed him. 'If anybody else but Kevin had approached me at that time, I wouldn't have considered it. You just don't say no to Heffo. And if you did, he wouldn't listen to you,' said the polished free taker.

Having given in to Kevin's persuasive appeal to return to the county team after a two-year lapse, Keaveney put himself through a rigorous schedule of training and a different lifestyle, far more demanding than any of his team colleagues. He was over 15 stone at the time. When the Leinster final came round, he was tipping the scales at 13 stone. But he was now a different kettle of fish, no longer the burly footballer of late. He was now a major figure-head, a vital cog in Heffernan's team plan for a provincial title. On 2 June at Pairc Tailteann, Navan, by coincidence the same ground on which he had played his last county game on 2 July 1972, Keaveney's presence at full forward proved masterly, not alone his accuracy from play and frees, but the manner in which he combined with the other forwards.

Kevin Heffernan stepped far more lightly leaving the Navan venue that Sunday after Dublin's 2-11 to 1-9 win over Louth. Offaly were fancied to stop them in the third round, but Dublin's new-found confidence saw them through on a 1-11 to 0-13 scoreline at Croke Park in a very close encounter. The men that Heffernan, Colfer and Redmond had moulded were now reaping the fruits of their labours. The Dublin following began to grow. The city needed a team to follow and the Dubs were now the big attraction, and winners too.

In those formative years Heffernan employed some basic tactics, learned during his own successful playing days. The idea was to draw out opposing full backs and make the space created pay dividends. But he wanted something a little more, a gambit that would assist his team to improve on marksmanship. He needed a central figure willing to carry out the ploy which was subsequently to change the whole face of Gaelic football. He knew the very man he wanted for that task — Tony Hanahoe, a skilful, clever forward who had the mental capacity to understand the tactic and the effect it was to have on the opposing defenders. Unselfishly, Hanahoe took over the role after many discussions with the team manager. The fact that he might disappear from the action of a game never worried him. He was thoroughly gratified to note that by taking the opposing centre back out of position, the other Dublin forwards would be able to attack and create openings for major scores. The ploy worked like a dream.

There was another item on Heffernan's shopping list which was 'a must'. He had

The 1974 Dublin All-Ireland champions. BACK ROW, LEFT TO RIGHT: *Stephen Rooney, Anton O'Toole, Robbie Kelleher, Jimmy Keaveney, Tony Hanahoe, Paddy Cullen, John McCarthy, Alan Larkin, Bobby Doyle.* FRONT ROW, LEFT TO RIGHT: *Brian Mullins, George Wilson, Paddy Reilly, Seán Doherty* (CAPTAIN), *David Hickey, Gay O'Driscoll.*

1974 All-Ireland action. FROM LEFT TO RIGHT: *C. McDonagh (Galway), T. Hanahoe (Dublin), B. Doyle (Dublin), L. Sammon (Galway), J. Keaveney (Dublin), J. Duggan (Galway), S. Doherty (Dublin), J. McCarthy (Dublin).*

to unearth physically endowed players who were capable of measuring up to the demands of stronger oppositions. A casual perusal of Heffernan's team indicated just that. Goalie Paddy Cullen topped the six foot mark. The full back line of Gay O'Driscoll, Seán Doherty and Robbie Kelleher followed suit. Alan Larkin at centre back dwarfed his wing men Paddy Reilly and Georgie Wilson, who were noted for their attacking forays. Brian Mullins and Steve Rooney were equal if not more formidable than any other midfield partnership at the time. Mullins, for his majestic fielding and positional play, ably abetted by Rooney's penchant for being in the right place at the right time and his excellent ball distribution, were a great midfield partnership. The Dublin attacking formation was perhaps the most lethal sector, dominated by the presence of Jimmy Keaveney at full forward, reaping the benefit of the space created by Hanahoe, with the in-rushing Anton O'Toole, David Hickey, Bobby Doyle and John McCarthy carving the openings for scores. Hovering in the background for future involvement were the names of Bernard Brogan and Pat O'Neill.

Heffernan left nothing to chance. The training routine devised by the Dublin team mentors differed greatly from any other system used by the Dublin teams of the past. There was a lot of emphasis on body-building, while the speed factor, always one of Heffernan's main priorities,

was never neglected at any time.

Early in May 1974, Dublin faced Kildare in the National League 'home final' at Croke Park. Admittedly, Dublin were only then emerging from the football doldrums at the time, and they lost an undistinguished encounter to the Lily Whites by a decisive seven-point margin. Some weeks later a better prepared Dublin team mounted a stiffer challenge to win their first championship outing against Wexford. The transition which followed beggared description. Thirteen of the side beaten by Kildare in the league encounter in early May now faced the Lily Whites in the semi-final of the Leinster championship. The Dublin support was huge; there was an old score to be settled.

There was a vast difference between the two protagonists for this important outing. Dublin were a far better drilled combination. They moved with greater authority and purpose from the outset. Anton O'Toole, who switched to midfield, worked like a Trojan and picked off some smart scores, while the half backs, who never rose to the occasion in the league game between the two teams in early May, were brilliantly led by Alan Larkin and ably supported by Paddy Reilly and Georgie Wilson. At the final whistle Dublin had won by 1-13 to 0-10.

More important still was the fact that Dublin had shown massive improvement from that opening game against Wexford.

The result was reflected in the confidence that filtered down through the team. The reaction of the by now huge Dublin following was gratifying to the ears of Heffernan, Colfer and Redmond. A big test was yet to come against old rivals, Meath, in the Leinster final.

So, after an interval of nine years Dublin were back again in a Leinster final, and their support had grown accordingly with Hill 16 now strictly the preserve of the Dublin supporters. Meath provided the opposition, but hopes of a closely fought encounter never materialised. More extraordinary still was the fact that Meath's Mickey Fay had the ball in the Dublin net after only 20 seconds. But this Dublin team was made of sterner stuff to be affected by that early snap score. Brian Mullins and Steve Rooney quickly established midfield dominance. The first half exchanges were riddled with frees, 43 in all. The play lacked continuity. Despite enjoying the advantage of a stiff breeze, Meath were only ahead 1-5 to 0-6 at half-time.

A tongue-lashing at the interval from manager Heffernan brought the desired results. Mullins and Rooney maintained their dominant role; Anton O'Toole swooped from both wings to create scores, while Paddy Reilly and the astute Tony Hanahoe fed the advancing Jimmy Keaveney for important scores. At the end of the day Dublin had regained the Leinster crown on a 1-14 to 1-9 scoreline. The Dubs were back in the All-Ireland race. The banners flew from the Hill: 'Deffo Heffo', 'The Dubs are back', 'Anto the Panther', and 'Here's to Sam' proclaimed that a new footballing force had arrived on the scene. Perhaps the most significant aspect of the Dublin win was that they had measured up physically and mentally to all the demands of a game which was not for the faint hearted. It must be stressed also that the Dublin side had weathered a very stiff Leinster campaign, displaying noticeable improvement in every round.

A true test of Dublin's progress would come against the defending champions, Cork, in the All-Ireland semi-final. I must confess to a degree of apprehension about the outcome of that clash at the time. I was amazed at the reaction of some of the players I interviewed for my column in the *Evening Press*. But there wasn't a shred of fear or doubt among the players about the outcome against Cork. They welcomed the chance and were quite confident. The Cork team, which included such great players as Jimmy Barry Murphy, Denis Coughlan, Declan Barron, Billy Morgan in goal, Ray Cummins and Humphrey Kelleher, just to mention some, had the capacity to capture another All-Ireland title — as seen through the eyes of most neutrals. Corner back Frank Cogan missed the game because of injury, but 14 of the All-Ireland winning team of 1973 were on duty. Among the statistics trotted out prior to the game were, that the counties had not met for 65 years and Cork had never beaten Dublin at championship level. Nevertheless this would be the ultimate test for the Dubs.

Another statistic, which may have been overlooked by the print media, was the display of Seán Doherty at full back. By no means the finished article when he was first introduced to the role, he nevertheless reeled off commendable displays throughout the Leinster campaign against the best full forwards in the game. His finest hour had yet to come.

The first of the All-Ireland semi-finals on 11 August brought an attendance of 42,190 to Croke Park. This turned out to be a tactical game and Cork had done their homework well. Strict marking was the order of the day, but Heffernan had anticipated that. He warned his team before the game that they had to be patient. Dublin still made use of Brian Mullins's forward forays, and the team responded by picking off some excellent points. Jimmy Barry Murphy was the prime danger man for Cork. He displayed his versatility midway through the first half when he was put clean through with only Paddy Cullen to beat in the Dublin goal. Cullen spread himself, narrowing the target, and Murphy's cracking effort struck the goal post and was cleared by Seán Doherty.

Dublin led 0-7 to 0-4 at the break. Prospects of an easy Dublin win were soon put on the back boiler after a succession of Dublin scoring chances were inexplicably missed. But for sterling work by the Dublin defence, Cork might well have got a grip on the game, but they were repulsed each time. In the 48th minute, Dublin produced a spectacular sequence of slick passing, which started from a brilliant midfield catch by Stephen Rooney. Tony Hanahoe was in position to receive a foot pass from Rooney, and he laid the ball on for John McCarthy. He slipped his marker and punted the ball to the unmarked Anton O'Toole, who cracked it to the Cork net. The Hill came alive. The Cork team mentors decided to make a change. The experienced Martin Doherty was summoned from the bench for duty. A very sound defender, he was sent in at full forward and Ned Kirby was signalled to make way for him.

Somewhere along the line the signals became crossed as play resumed. Kirby remained on the field while Doherty took his place at full forward. Cork had now 16 players on the field. Dublin protested to the referee, but before action was taken Doherty was fouled in the square and Cork were awarded a penalty, stroked to the Dublin net by Jimmy Barry Murphy. Meanwhile, Cork hauled off Ned Kirby and that ended Cork's numerical advantage. The match really came alive then and Dublin set about restoring their grip on the game. The roving Bobby Doyle and the accuracy of Steve Rooney helped to put more daylight between the

1975 All-Ireland football final, Dublin v Kerry. FROM LEFT TO RIGHT: *John McCarthy (Dublin) punches the ball over the head of Ger O'Keeffe (Kerry) as Paddy Gogarty (Dublin no. 15) looks on. Ogie Moran (Kerry) is in the background.*

Dublin All-Ireland champions 1976. BACK ROW, LEFT TO RIGHT: *Kevin Moran, Anton O'Toole, Seán Doherty, Jimmy Keaveney, Paddy Cullen, John McCarthy, Tom Drumm, Bernard Brogan, Bobby Doyle.* FRONT ROW, LEFT TO RIGHT: *Brian Mullins, Robbie Kelleher, Pat O'Neill, Tony Hanahoe, David Hickey, Gay O'Driscoll.*

The 1976 All-Ireland football final. FROM LEFT TO RIGHT: *Denis Moran (Kerry), Robbie Kelleher (Dublin), Mike Sheehy (Kerry).*

teams. The clincher came in the final quarter when Jimmy Keaveney was fouled in the square and Brian Mullins coolly slotted the resultant penalty home. Mullins had a good penalty record that year. He scored from the spot against Louth, Kildare and Cork in turn. For the record, Mullins's goal against Cork was unique, being the first penalty goal award for a Leinster team in a semi-final since 1963, when John Timmons pointed one for Dublin against

Down. It was also the first goal from the penalty spot in an All-Ireland senior semi-final for six years.

When the referee blew the final whistle Dublin were the winners by 2-11 to Cork's 1-8. Close on 220,000 spectators saw Dublin's championship run in 1974. The crowd of 42,190 fans at the semi-final was the biggest at this stage of the competition since the introduction of the 80-minute game in 1970.

Once again careful attention to detail helped bring the city men along a proverbial ton. The tight-marking defensive set-up of O'Driscoll, Doherty and Kelleher, backed by the solidity of Paddy Cullen's goalkeeping, had fashioned one of the best defences in football at that time. The key also lay in the formidable back bone down the middle of Doherty, Larkin, Mullins, Hanahoe and Keaveney. Kevin Heffernan's dream of football dominance among the country's best would soon be put to the test on All-Ireland final day against Galway on 22 September at Croke Park.

There had been an uneasy relationship between the GAA and the New York GAA board for many years and it affected the inclusion of New York at championship and league involvement. Relations between New York and the Central Council took a nosedive in October 1970, following a vicious attack on Dublin referee Clem Foley, one of the best and most competent officials operating at that time. It happened after the National Hurling League final between Cork and New York at Gaelic Park. It was a disgraceful incident. Foley, who had refereed the game to everybody's satisfaction, was struck by a spectator as he was leaving the pitch. He was hospitalised for three days and had to undergo surgery for a facial injury. GAA president Pat Fanning loudly condemned the incident and following the reading of the referee's report John Maher and John Lynch were expelled from the association. The Clem Foley incident was to start a chain reaction of events which saw the banning of all visits to New York in 1971 by teams from this country until January 1972. In January 1971 the executive committee of the GAA granted an application for two teams to play in the Cardinal Cushing Games in May, provided the restrictions placed on the games in Gaelic Park, New York, were observed. At the Offaly convention held in February, the board president Fr E. Vaughan proposed that they send two club football teams to play in the Cushing Games, and this was passed.

I was a member of the Cardinl Cushing Games committee and I accepted that a ban had been placed on counties travelling to and playing in New York. I was a personal friend of John Kerry O'Donnell, so I phoned him and suggested that he take out the Jimmy Magee All-Stars plus showband personalities to play for the Cardinal Cushing Games charity in New York and Boston. It proved the way out of the dilemma, and John Kerry jumped at the idea. I was a member of the Jimmy Magee troupe which had played in charity matches, raising vast sums of money for local charities in Ireland and in England. The secret of the Magee All-Stars lay in the fact that it was comprised of former great players who had become household names and who were still able to command followings at the charity matches. The Magee All-Stars flew to New York on 21 May that year. The party included Seán Purcell and Frankie Stockwell (Galway), Christy Ring (Cork), John Nallen (Mayo), Gerry O'Malley (Roscommon), Frankie Byrne (Meath), Dermot O'Brien (Louth), Larry Cunningham (Longford), Fr Mick Cleary (Dublin), Kevin Armstrong (Antrim), Willie Casey (Mayo), and John Dowling and Paddy Kennedy (Kerry).

Jimmy Magee was in charge and Liam Campbell was there giving his usual match commentary. The biggest attendance ever turned up at Gaelic Park on 23 May, billed as 'Oldtimers' Day', to watch the former stars in action. In the words of John Kerry O'Donnell afterwards, it was a case of 'doing it without ruffling the extremely

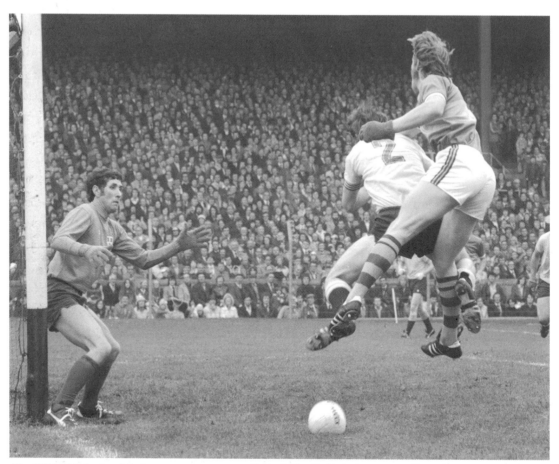

The 1977 All-Ireland semi-final. FROM LEFT TO RIGHT: *Paddy Cullen (Dublin), Gay O'Driscoll (Dublin), Pat Spillane (Kerry). Paddy Cullen is alert to the danger.*

sensitive fine feathers of authority'. The whole operation was one of the most enjoyable and successful Magee All-Stars charity occasions. As instigator of the trip, I was unable to go with the travelling party, but I was delighted to have been involved in its arrangement.

In October 1971, the Central Council approved a recommendation by the executive committee, after consultation with New York GAA board officers in Dublin, to lift the suspension imposed on John Maher for the alleged attack on Clem Foley and allow him to play in New York competitions. On 9 January 1972, John Kerry O'Donnell was elected president of the New York GAA and in his election speech said that they should co-operate with the Central Council in every possible way in endeavouring to put relations between the council and New York on a more harmonious footing. The wheel had come full circle again.

In 1969 an Antrim motion to congress asked that a special commission be set up to investigate the GAA's affairs under eight headings: structure, finance, youth, grounds, communications, hurling, discipline and sponsorship. It represented the most exhaustive self-analysis by a volunteer organisation ever undertaken in this country, and ultimately led to a radical overhaul of the GAA's administrative machine. To ensure the independence of the commission, about half of its members were from outside the GAA. It included leading figures in both public and private sectors of industry.

The report was accepted as a blueprint for the GAA of the 1970s and 80s. It discussed various factors believed to be impeding progress, and devised a scheme for restructuring the GAA which would enable it to meet the challenges it would have to face for the rest of the century. The association's weaknesses were analysed and the extent to which new techniques could advance the GAA's interests were considered. The most far-reaching changes suggested by the commission concerned the administrative structure of the GAA. Future central councils should, the report suggested, meet only quarterly and have a mainly overseeing function.

Between congresses the association's affairs should be handled by a management committee answerable to the council. The programme of games and other events should be taken over by a new activities committee; the general development of the association should be controlled by a central development committee working to the management committee. To emphasise his enhanced status in a restructured GAA, the general secretary should in future be known as the director-general. He should be supported by a management accountant (actually appointed by the time the report appeared), an activities officer, a central development officer and a public relations officer.

The longest chapter in the commission's report dealt with the vital subject of communications. Among the topics investigated were the improvement of contacts with the press, the coverage of Gaelic games on television, the feasibility of producing films on coaching, the future of the *Our Games* annual, and the publication of year books and youth magazines. Surprisingly, in view of later developments in this field, sponsorship received only three pages in the entire report: it produced the only reservation. Tomas Roseingrave of Muintir na Tire disapproved of sponsorship by cigarette manufacturers of an athletic body like the GAA, a view which has since found wide support throughout the association.

On grounds, the commission had little new to say. A comprehensive record and a valuation of each stadium, and a more effective system of control to safeguard the association's interests, were recommended. Future expenditure should aim at improving existing grounds; every main county ground should have covered accommodation and a first-aid room. The 60,000 word document ran to 140 pages.

On 22 September 1974, 71,898 spectators packed Croke Park and watched the Dublin footballers claim their 18th All-Ireland senior crown, beating Galway 0-14 to 1-6. Dublin's rags to riches story ended 11 years of frustration at top football level. But thanks to the hard work and unbridled enthusiasm on the part of Kevin Heffernan and his co-selectors, Donal Colfer and Lorcan Redmond, the team they had moulded enacted the football miracle of the age. Paddy Downey summed up the occasion succinctly in his after-match report in *The Irish Times* the following day.

As hordes of people, some downcast in defeat, the greater number exultant in victory, travelled along the Dublin quays, on wheels and on foot, at 5.30 yesterday evening, the Liffey lapped its walls in full flood, tide meeting river to close the eyes of bridges. It seemed as if nature had chosen that hour, or that moment, to offer a gesture of harmony with the scene at Croke Park only three-quarters of an hour before, when the Dublin football team, also in full flood, defeated Galway by five points in the 88th All-Ireland final.

Their victory was memorable, their winning margin large enough to extinguish all doubts, all arguments, at the finish. But, alas, the quality of the game did not gild the great occasion for Seán Doherty's team. Dublin's first All-Ireland title since 1963 and their 18th in all deserved something better to

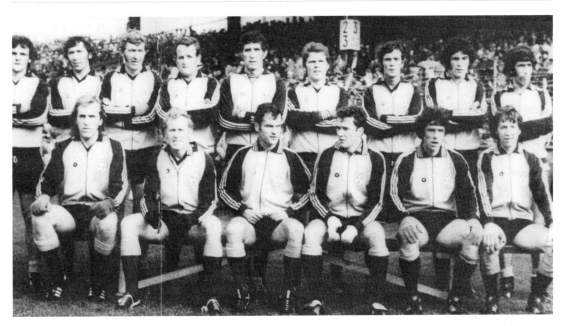

The 1978 All-Ireland football final. BACK ROW, LEFT TO RIGHT: *Kevin Moran, Anton O'Toole, Seán Doherty, Jimmy Keaveney, Paddy Cullen, Tommy Drumm, John McCarthy, Bernard Brogan, Bobby Doyle.* FRONT ROW, LEFT TO RIGHT: *Brian Mullins, Pat O'Neill, Tony Hanahoe* (CAPTAIN), *David Hickey, Robbie Kelleher, Gay O'Driscoll.*

The 1978 All-Ireland final. FROM LEFT TO RIGHT: *Jack O'Shea (Kerry), Robbie Kelleher (Dublin).*

The 1978 All-Ireland final. FROM LEFT TO RIGHT: *Brian Mullins (Dublin), Pat O'Neill (Dublin), Eoin Liston (Kerry), Seán Doherty (Dublin).*

adorn memory in the years to come.

How rash it is to prophesy great spectacles. Both teams were caught in the grip of tension from the start, and while it diminished a little as time passed, that tension never eased out. Fouls of many hues riddled the game,

snipping continuity on average every 87 seconds and ruling out the fluent, polished football that so many had unrealistically expected.

One of the prime danger men in the Galway attack was undoubtedly corner forward Johnny Tobin, who was in devastating form, having scored 2-5 in his side's dismissal of Donegal in the All-Ireland semi-final. Tobin's name went into Heffernan's notebook along with other names who posed a threat to Dublin's survival. Heffernan believed in doing his homework.

Gay O'Driscoll clamped handcuffs on danger man Tobin, completely isolating him from the action, and denying him space and service from the outfield. Shrewd roving forays by Anton O'Toole and David Hickey, securing possession from the rewards of great midfield fetching by Brian Mullins and Steve Rooney, kept the pressure on the Galway defensive cover. Jimmy Keaveney, alert and sharp, picked off eight points, some from frees, to add to his remarkable championship tally. The defining moment for Dublin came 13 minutes into the second half.

Galway pressure was mounting when they launched an attack, and as Liam Sammon stretched for the ball he was hauled to the ground. Referee Patsy Devlin (Tyrone) immediately pointed to the penalty spot. The situation was crucial for both teams at that moment. A Galway goal from the penalty would put the Connacht men in a very sound position. A miss would strengthen the resolve of the Dublin team.

Liam Sammon was the Galway penalty taker. Goalie Paddy Cullen had his mind made up about his intentions. He told me after that match that he had watched Sammon taking other penalties for Galway. 'I noticed that he invariably favoured putting the ball to the goalkeeper's left-hand side, head high. That helped my concentration. I was willing Liam to place the ball to my left and I dived that way when the shot came in. I was lucky as I got the tips of my fingers to the ball and deflected it out for a 50.' Cullen's brilliant save was in effect a match-winner. In the closing 13 minutes, points from Jimmy Keaveney, Brian Mullins and David Hickey won the game for the home county, whose superior technical skill, enthusiasm and ardour would not have been exaggerated by a far wider winning total. I believe Galway were nonplussed at times by the frequency or constancy with which the Dublin attack, especially, interchanged positions. The pity was that the contest had to fall so far below expectations. Galway never moved with the expected sharpness they had shown in previous games. They appeared to wait to see if things would happen. In Dublin's case, they made things happen — the prime difference between two great battling teams. So once again the wily head of Kevin Heffernan brought back lustre and pride to the capital city and to the loyal Dublin supporters who now had an outlet to express their true feelings. A new era beckoned which would be known as 'the glory years'.

The early 1970s brought to a close the careers of two powerful figures of influence in Church and State in the Republic. Éamon de Valera ended his second term of the presidency in June 1973, completing over sixty years in Irish public life. He died on 29 August 1975. Dr John Charles McQuaid was replaced in February 1972 after 32 years as Archbishop of Dublin. He died on 7 April 1973. The two men had been friends since the late 1920s and that friendship had survived the conflicts and the confrontations of Church and State during the 1940s and 50s.

Both men had, in their respective ways, shaped modern Ireland in the mould of Catholic nationalism. De Valera's life had been interwoven with the pattern of Irish history for half a century. His official biographers have underlined his devotion to principle, the supreme importance to him of his religious faith, his attachment to democracy, his role as a constitutionalist, his belief in republicanism, and his sense of nationality.

When Dr McQuaid was appointed Archbishop of Dublin in 1940, he became a vigorous upholder of the authority and place of the Catholic Church in the public sphere. During his time as archbishop, he expanded Church influence in education, in the social services, and in the area of the voluntary hospitals. In the early 1950s he successfully fought to prevent the application of a welfare state in Ireland. He built new churches and greatly strengthened the institutional Church. He left behind a social service structure which, although partly funded by the exchequer, operated beyond its control. McQuaid and de Valera, therefore, lived long enough to witness a changing society over which neither could exercise any further guidance or control.

Both the Irish State and the Catholic Church were unprepared for the pace of the change that characterised the 1960s and 70s. McQuaid and de Valera were very much products of more innocent and naive times. Industrialisation brought in its wake greater urbanisation and the mass relocation of the Irish population, especially to Dublin. In 1972 Fianna Fáil had been in power for 15 consecutive years. Jack Lynch had become Taoiseach in 1966, only to witness the radical deterioration of the political situation in Northern Ireland. That, in turn, contributed to the outbreak of virtual 'civil war' within Fianna Fáil in 1969/70, leading to the removal/resignation from the cabinet of the Minister for Finance, Charles J. Haughey, and others. The 'Arms Trial' followed, the outcome of which had significant long-term consequences for the leadership of Jack Lynch and for his wing of Fianna Fáil.

Lynch, wrongly perceived as a weak leader, had the firmness in 1970 to impose unity on the party from above with manageable losses of personnel — even if those losses involved the scions of two of the most important republican families, Kevin Boland and Neil Blaney. Charles Haughey, condemned to the back benches, never deemed that to be a permanent state bestowed upon him by providence. His rightful place — and that of his wing of the party — was in the vanguard of Fianna Fáil, and he surprised many by replacing Jack Lynch as leader in 1979. Sir John Peck, the British Ambassador in Dublin between 1970 and 1973, wrote of Jack Lynch in his memoirs: 'All those concerned with, and committed

The 1979 All-Ireland final. FROM LEFT TO RIGHT: *John Egan (Kerry), Seán Doherty (Dublin), Tommy Drumm (Dublin).*

Dublin footballers training in Parnell Park, including Mick Hickey, John Caffrey, Jim Roynane, Bernard Brogan, Mick Holden and Mick Kennedy.

to, peace with justice in the North owe a very great deal to his courage and tenacity in pursuing what he believed to be the right policy. . . . I do not think that I ever succeeded in convincing British politicians of how much we owed him at that stage, or what the consequences would have been if he had lost his head.'

Dublin's 1974 All-Ireland success was to bring its own reward, apart altogether from the honour and glory aspect which rightly belonged to the players and the team officials. But Dublin's entry into the ranks of the great brought an amazing transformation in the people's attitude towards them, bordering on hero worship. No Dublin football team was ever the subject of such media concentration as 'Heffo's heroes'. And there were a number of reasons for that. The Dublin sporting public had at last a winning team to follow. English soccer stars who were held up as idols were soon replaced by the Dubs, and names like Cullen, Doyle, Keaveney, O'Toole, Mullins, Hickey, O'Driscoll and

Doherty were quickly identified as the new heroes in the minds of the city sports followers.

The travelling supporters, with their decorative banners and flags, began to appear all over the country where the Dubs were playing, and in greater numbers than ever before. In spite of the huge regular following whose conduct was exemplary, they also had to contend with a small group who were followers in name only, who looked on Gaelic football as a game played by 'country fellas', and who stepped outside the canons of good behaviour on occasions at away fixtures.

The phoenix-like rise of the Dublin football team changed all that. The euphoria created by Heffernan in bringing Dublin out of the football wilderness kept the momentum going. However, Dublin's defeat by Kerry in 1975 proved a crushing blow for a team which had set its sights on more glory on All-Ireland day. Kerry came to Croke Park better trained than any previous Kerry team. Their manager, Mick O'Dwyer, had gained a valuable insight into Dublin's *modus operandi* following their success against Galway. Kerry training for the 1975 All-Ireland placed greater emphasis on fitness, at a level they had not reached previously. It was that factor which enabled Kerry to stay with Dublin through all the tense periods of that physical encounter. Kerry's tactical plan was cleverly fashioned. Danger man Mikey Sheehy started at full forward, normally a winger or corner forward. Denis 'Ogie' Moran, a splendid half back, was moved to centre forward. Mick O'Dwyer needed a strong midfielder to offset the Brian Mullins/Bernard Brogan powerful Dublin duo. The surprise choice turned out to be Pat McCarthy, who had been playing his club football in Kildare. But he was a strong, direct player and his selection turned out to be a master stroke. McCarthy and Paud Lynch dominated the centre of the field to such an extent that the Kerry forwards got a virtual non-stop supply of the ball, which was to pave the way ultimately for their 2-12 to 0-11 victory. Kerry captain Mickey O'Sullivan, who played a magnificent part in his team's triumph was felled by a Seán Doherty elbow as he came charging through on a surging run. He didn't learn until much later of his team's success as he had been taken to hospital following that incident.

Heffernan, Colfer and Redmond sat down after that defeat with a film of the final to seek answers to a few problems that arose from that game. They concentrated on the defence which leaked like a sieve. The half back line was obviously going to be the focus of much attention. What appeared good enough and accomplished enough the previous year when winning the All-Ireland suddenly looked in need of immediate repair.

I remember having chats with the three team officials from time to time about the team's performances. Their three-man selector set-up had established a new trend and did away with the old-fashioned, overloaded team of selectors. In all the years in which Heffernan, Colfer and Redmond were in charge of Dublin teams, there were never any stand-offs or rows over individual selections. Donal Colfer once told me: 'There was never any reason for rows. The three of us knew the type of player needed for a certain position. We always made sure that our final choice would come through our training spins at Parnell Park. Lorcan would watch talent in the Fingal area and I watched potentials operating on the south and west city, while Kevin would look at north city talent.' Donal was at O'Toole Park watching Good Counsel play Civil Service in the St Vincent de Paul tournament and was very impressed with a young Good Counsel midfielder, who was constantly out-fielding taller opponents among the opposition. The young man was Kevin Moran. Donal asked him to turn up for training with the Dubs at Parnell Park the following Tuesday night.

The same invitation was offered to Tommy Drumm, and to Pat O'Neill who had already seen a bit of action with the Dubs during the 1975 championship mainly as a substitute. 'It was always our policy,' said Donal Colfer, 'to have a panel in place that would have the potential to win an All-Ireland and to have guys suitable enough who would subsequently make the grade at top level.' Kevin Moran was an exception to the rule. When he turned up for his first training stint at Parnell Park, he was so much at home playing against the big names that he looked as if he had always been part of the regular team panel. Drumm, Moran and O'Neill would be the big Dublin team players in the year ahead when the All-Ireland (and Kerry) would be the prime objective.

In the 1970s a major effort got under way on a 32-county scale to expand the area where hurling of a standard comparable to that of the leading counties would be achieved. The objective of the 20-year hurling scheme, prepared in 1964, was to have hurling in every parish in Ireland by centenary year 1984. It was a bold plan. Originally the scheme was divided into four 5-year periods. Between 1964 and 1969 each county was to set up a hurling committee to implement the scheme. A central hurling committee would administer grants and ensure supplies of hurleys. Counties were to be graded, hurleys to be distributed in bulk, annual coaching courses organised, and a special fund to be built up by a levy on certain matches.

The specific aim of the 1965–69 plan, participation by 1969 of all 32 counties in the minor championship, was achieved.

Nearly 200,000 juvenile hurleys were supplied during the life of the plan. To promote weaker counties to the average sector and average ones to the strong sector, a novel scheme of county adoption was devised involving visits and demonstrations by counties in one group to those in a lower group. Progress tended to be uneven: for some years an acute shortage of adult hurleys was encountered. In general, the results suggested that what the Rackard brothers had done for Wexford in the 1950s would not easily be repeated elsewhere except over a much longer period of time and through exceptionally persistent dedication.

The political turmoil in the North had understandably affected the GAA. The spread of civil unrest from 1968 and the subsequent violence naturally made life more difficult for the association. Not only

The 1979 All-Ireland final. Mike Sheehy (Kerry) shoots for goal. Dublin players Fran Ryder, Tommy Drumm and Mick Kennedy are in the background.

did it suffer from the periodic disruption of normal life, its members were among those harassed by a partisan police force, pursued by a biased legal machine and imprisoned without trial. Since the fall of Stormont in 1972 the GAA has received special attention from the British forces which, with the approval of the government, have occupied and damaged GAA property in several places, notably the major stadium at Casement Park, Belfast, and the GAA grounds at Crossmaglen. Repeated protests, including a meeting in London in 1971 between the GAA chief officers and a member of the British Government, have not reduced the provocation offered to a body whose only offence in British eyes can be its advocacy of a united Ireland.

When funds to relieve distress in Northern Ireland were badly needed, the GAA south of the border acted speedily and effectively. As early as 1972 the central council had collected and distributed £80,000 for this purpose. When harmony is ultimately restored between the two communities in the North, the GAA may face a new problem there. With the vital necessity to build bridges between the opposing cultures, the association may anticipate pressure for a contribution towards the strengthening of that harmony from a body with such potential for good community relations. It is good to see our President, Mary McAleese, and husband Martin using their position to build bridges in many ways between communities in the South and in the North, and long may it continue.

The GAA's achievement in the past century give grounds for the expectation of even greater success in the future. It arrested an important aspect of the peaceful penetration of Ireland by English culture and began the cultural revival which led to the political revolution of the 1913–1922 period, in which it played a major role. It saved the principal native games from extinction.

Kevin Heffernan's reaction to the 1975 defeat was one of regret that his side had not produced the same level of performance which had marked their previous year's success. He blamed the long, hard slog of the two years of stiff training, the constant pile of fixtures which had to be fulfilled, the ever-demanding media, the pressures of business and home and the normal pressures that the big occasion brings on the playing fields. Kerry had by far the easier passage coming out of Munster, a one-sided win over Sligo in the All-Ireland semi-final (3-13 to 0-5), whereas Dublin were stretched to beat Derry 3-13 to 3-8 in their penultimate round. Heffernan was quoted as saying, 'Right through the year the Dublin players gave every bit as much in training and in preparation, but the marginal reduction in fire was enough to make the difference against Kerry.' Heffernan, Colfer and Redmond vowed that the mistakes made in 1975 would not be repeated, and by the time the 1976 championship season arrived, the mood in the Dublin camp was vastly different. It was down to business in a big way.

The players knew in their hearts that their 1975 performance on the day was as dismal as the weather in which it was played. There were no recriminations among the players; very few of them measured up to the demands of the test. Credit was duly paid to Kerry for their extraordinary win. Everything they attempted had a touch of class. They teamed and schemed together. They punished Dublin in areas where the Dubs appeared untouchable. Heffernan kept his powder dry, a man not given to publicly criticising his own players. He was well aware that the old fire was missing, but more important still was his gut feeling that the time had come for some structural changes. But it was not a time for the wholesale dismembering of a team which had brought glory back to the county just a year before.

Heffernan, Colfer and Redmond were on the same wavelength about one thing: the sooner the Dublin players got back into action, the sooner the plans being formulated could be put into practice. The league was to provide the vehicle for this important restoration of confidence and hunger among the players, and for those getting a first call-up to action. Alan Larkin, who had given the county Trojan service at centre half back, opted out, and Pat O'Neill was slotted in for the trip to the Mardyke for the opening league tie against Cork.

Dublin's preparations for the Leeside visit helped them in a big way. The loyal fans again filled the venue and the team responded with a display which lifted the gloom that followed the defeat by the Kingdom a few months earlier. There was now fire in their bellies. The slackness and uncertainty of another time and place were quickly replaced with an iron resolve and a confident attitude. No matter how hard a formidable Cork side tried, they were unable to break down a fully tuned up Dublin defence. Nor indeed could Cork match the brilliance of the Dublin attacking formation. Dublin went on to win 1-12 to 1-4. The big one was ahead of them. Their next outing was against old rivals, Kerry. Writing in his *Irish Press* match report the following day, my good friend Pádraig Puirséal summed it up concisely when he stated: 'For speed, thrills, scintillating passages of combined play and feats of individual brilliance it would be hard to beat the entertainment produced during the opening 30 minutes. The two teams had richly earned the prolonged applause that followed them to their half-time dressing rooms from the crowd which was in excess of 25,000.' Puirséal and the other sports writers marvelled at the performance served up by Brian Mullins in that match. He dictated the flow of play at midfield, he was back helping out in defence and added gainfully to the attacking forays. The team responded and Dublin assumed an edge they never relinquished.

Allowing for Kerry's inevitable stints of celebrations following their 1975 success over the Dubs, they still came to Croke Park fully determined to maintain their dominance over their city rivals. Enthusiasm wasn't enough, as Dublin won the match deservedly on a 2-11 to 0-13 scoreline. It was a verdict which pleased Heffernan, Colfer and Redmond very much. More important still was the effect it had on 'Heffo's army'. They revelled in the outcome which helped to regain a lot of fallen pride. Wins over Kildare and Offaly, despite a shock defeat at the hands of Roscommon, saw Dublin through to the National League semi-final against Galway.

Unfortunately, that game never reached expectations on 4 April 1976. Both teams suffered from inaccurate shooting, none more so than Galway. They came out of the traps like a flash, and for most of the first half they enjoyed ample possession, but efforts at scores turned into nightmares. The display by the Dublin defenders in allowing the Galway forwards the freedom of the pitch was alarming. A half-time tongue-lashing had the right effect. Dublin grabbed the game by the scruff of the neck. The turning point came when Tony Hanahoe was beautifully played into a scoring position by Kevin Moran, and the shrewd St Vincent's player slammed the ball home. Dublin's second half display had power written all over it and they emerged winners narrowly enough by 1-11 to 0-12. Hanahoe's goal proved the clincher.

The National League final between Dublin and Derry was watched by 33,845 spectators at Croke Park. The Ulster men came with a huge reputation. It was an ideal opportunity for the Dublin selectors to give some of their fringe players a chance to show their mettle. The old reliable back line of Paddy Cullen (goalie), Gay O'Driscoll, Seán Doherty and Robbie Kelleher remained intact. Pat O'Neill at centre back had new flankers in Brendan Pocock and Kevin Synnott, both of whom had already played in the course of the league. The game turned into a cliff-hanger that few had anticipated. Derry made all the running, with Gerry McElhinny, Anthony McGurk, Micky Lynch, Seán O'Connell and Brendan Kelly using the good supply from Tom McGuinness and Séamus Lagan at midfield to race into a five-point lead. O'Connell, playing in his third final since making his debut in 1957, was particularly brilliant. Five minutes from the interval, Paddy Gogarty, a lion-hearted performer,

The 1979 All-Ireland final. FROM LEFT TO RIGHT: *Mick Holden (Dublin), Eoin Liston (Kerry), Paddy Cullen (Dublin). Liston punches for a Kerry point.*

lifted the Dublin gloom when he rounded the Derry defence, after a great pass from Jimmy Keaveney, to smash home a terrific goal. Dublin were back in business.

Derry dominated the early stages of the second half, with Fintan McCloskey now at midfield instead of Séamus Lagan, but Dublin were not to be outdone. Bobby Doyle, Anton O'Toole, Jimmy Keaveney and David Hickey were finding the range, and Keaveney did, what he invariably does best when he caught the Derry defence on the wrong foot. He had his sights set on the space between himself and Derry goalie Mark McFeeley, and despite the pressure, fired home a cracking goal in the 45th minute. Derry managed to go in front again until they conceded the lead score to David Hickey who, along with Kevin Moran, scored two points. Moran's midfield performance was captivating and he teamed up brilliantly with Brian Mullins, especially in the second half when Dublin had it all to do to win narrowly 2-10 to 0-15. Once again Paddy Cullen, Gay O'Driscoll and Robbie Kelleher edged it in defence. David Hickey, Anton O'Toole and the remarkable Jimmy Keaveney, who headed the scoring table with 3-19 in the series, took the attacking honours.

Dublin counted themselves lucky to have survived a game which Derry conceivably should have won. It was Dublin's fourth league title and they went on to capture the honours again in 1978, 87, 91 and 93. The Heffernan, Colfer,

Redmond triumvirate achieved three All-Ireland senior football titles and two National League crowns, a magnificent tally, sometimes against all the odds. (Gerry McElhinney was later to make his name with Bolton Wanderers and Northern Ireland in soccer, while Kevin Moran would win 70 international soccer caps with the Republic of Ireland between 1980 and 94 while playing with Manchester United.)

I remember discussing Dublin's league title success with Donal Colfer some weeks afterwards and he agreed that the side was extremely lucky to have taken the honours. There were several very promising under-21 players taking part in domestic competitions at the time, players who appeared to me to have strong credentials for inclusion in the county team. I asked Donal about their prospects of getting into the side. His reply amazed me. 'How could we drop players who have won three All-Ireland titles and two National League crowns, and are still playing top-class football?' Kerry were still the popular choice when preparations began for the 1976 championship. The league crown was just the lift Dublin needed. Kevin Heffernan was already planning the Kingdom's downfall though he wouldn't admit it at the time.

With the 1976 National League won, the road to Leinster championship honours started with a trip to Mullingar to play Longford, which I remembered as the day Kevin Moran was slotted in at centre forward in place of the injured captain Tony Hanahoe. A few weeks earlier Tony had suffered a broken elbow. Moran, given his big chance, proceeded to grasp it with both hands. He led the Dublin attack in masterly fashion, creating and finishing scores himself. O'Connor Park, Tullamore, was next on the list and the opposition was provided by Laois. Back in his central role at centre forward was Tony Hanahoe. Highlight of that match was the great display by Tommy Drumm at wing back. The Dublin midfield got a bit of a roasting from Bobby Burns and Kieran Brennan, but after leading 0-10 to 1-6 at the break the Laois attack could only muster one point in the second period. Dublin, through Jimmy Keaveney, Paddy Gogarty and Anton O'Toole, added 3-12.

It was Meath then in the Leinster final. The failure by Colm O'Rourke to score from a penalty 17 minutes before the finish proved a costly miss. Dublin, against the run of play, emerged victors once again by 2-8 to 1-9.

Kevin Moran, who had sustained an injured shoulder in the Leinster final, reported fit for the All-Ireland semi-final against Galway. This proved another disappointing occasion. The football was dour and dogged and the emphasis was on spoiling tactics. It must be said that Dublin produced the better football in a match that had 67 frees awarded. The abiding memory of that contest was the vital

Dublin goal, scored 20 minutes into the second half, which proved crucial. Gay O'Driscoll started the movement after a quick intercept and laid off to Robbie Kelleher. Bernard Brogan and Brian Mullins were next to combine, and a swift pass to Bobby Doyle sent the St Vincent's man on a speedy solo run. Jimmy Keaveney was waiting on the fringe of the square when the ball reached him. Keaveney moved slightly to the left, threw his marker off balance and cracked the ball to the net with his right boot. That was to be Galway's swan-song.

Once again the display from Tommy Drumm was one of the talking points of Dublin's success, ably backed by the no-nonsense Pat O'Neill, whose reputation was growing, and the central figure in the half line, Kevin Moran. It was that trio which broke the back of the Galway challenge and the line which was to mastermind further glory for the Dubs in the final.

A few surprising facts emerged from the Dublin-Galway semi-final which were unknown to the public. There was concern in the Dublin camp about Brian Mullins who had not produced the form expected. It was discovered that Brian played for most of the match with a fractured jaw. However, it wasn't so serious as to prevent him from turning out in a challenge game against Down a fortnight later. Paddy Gogarty, who had an excellent game against Laois in the Leinster semi-final, retained his place for the Leinster final against Meath. Gogarty had missed the All-Ireland semi-final against Galway because of a broken bone in his hand, which led to the recall of John McCarthy to corner forward, while Tommy Drumm displaced Paddy Reilly on the half back line.

There was much speculation in the city about the composition of the Dublin side for the 1976 All-Ireland football final. Kerry, as expected, opted for the 15 who had beaten Dublin the year before. In some of the pre-match interviews with the Dublin players, they were consistent in their views that Kerry were going to be very hard to beat. They emphasised the strong qualities of the Kingdom side. It looked as if Kerry had nothing to do but turn up and the Sam Maguire cup was theirs.

Neutral followers plunged their money on Kerry to win back-to-back titles. Dublin delayed their final line-out. Heffernan had the players straining at the bit in their training quarters, which were changed frequently. Kerry manager Mick O'Dwyer had his own problems. Corner backs Ger O'Keefe and Jimmy Deenihan were suffering from aggravated ankle injuries picked up in their semi-final win over Derry. Goalkeeper Paud Mahony was troubled by a strained Achilles tendon and was genuinely a source of major worry in the Kerry camp. The build-up to the final was given massive coverage. The injury worries on both sides were buried deep under the avalanche of match comments by the print media, while RTÉ had cameras covering every aspect of the eagerly awaited clash of the two footballing powers. When Dublin released their team, the half back line was comprised of Tommy Drumm, Kevin Moran and Pat O'Neill.

There was some apprehension in Dublin football circles about the presence of the two youngsters, Drumm and Moran, for such an important tie, having only played together as a line for the first time in the semi-final against Galway. O'Neill was a seasoned defender from UCD who had made a remarkable recovery from a serious illness a couple of years before. But these half backs had blotted out Galway's highly rated half forwards. Kerry manager Mick O'Dwyer rightly feared their influence on the team.

The 1976 All-Ireland football final will be remembered for a lot of important reasons. RTÉ beamed the game to New York, Chicago, Boston, San Francisco, Pittsburgh, Toronto, London, Coventry, Birmingham, Northampton, Slough and many other venues where the game was shown to packed halls and public houses. The interest shown by the general public for the meeting of the great rivals was unbelievable. The attendance of 73,588 set a new record for GAA headquarters since

The 1979 All-Ireland final. FROM LEFT TO RIGHT: *Mick Kennedy (Dublin), Eoin Liston (Kerry), Mick Holden (Dublin), Mike Sheehy (Kerry), Fran Ryder (Dublin).*

the capacity of the ground had been reduced at the end of the 1965 season. The game started in sensational fashion after referee Paddy Collins (Westmeath) had thrown the ball in. Dublin captain Tony Hanahoe had won the toss and opted to play into the Railway goal. Young Kevin Moran, in his first final but completely unphased by the occasion, came ranging up from centre back. He careered past midfield, through the Kerry defence, took a return pass from Bernard Brogan and then fired in a cracking shot that flew inches wide of the goal post. Had it found its mark, it would have been the greatest score ever in an All-Ireland final.

Moran's upfield dash took about forty seconds, but it lit a Dublin fire which Kerry were unable to quench. The scoreline read at the finish: Dublin 3-8, Kerry 0-10. Pádraig Puirséal, in his report on the game the following day in the *Irish Press*, said:

'I'd rather be a Jack than a King', announced one of the myriad banners that waved so proudly over the massed battalions of Heffo's Army on the Croke Park Hill, but to be accurate, every Dublin player out there on the pitch was a King of Football as the Boys in Blue so convincingly dethroned the Kerry champions and thus achieved a victory every Dubliner will treasure for the rest of his life. Nor could any success have possibly been sweeter.

Dublin avenged last year's defeat by dethroning the 1975 Kings from the Kingdom; they beat Kerry in the championship for the first time since 1934, and in a final for the first time since 1923 . . . and as every football fan from the 31 counties knows, as Peter McDermott from Meath said when receiving the Sam Maguire Cup in 1954, 'Beating Kerry in a final counts two to the rest of us.'

The strategy conjured up by the Dublin selectors never varied one iota. Even the fact that Bobby Doyle had suffered a hamstring injury in training never reached the outside world as the 'Doyler' battled to regain fitness. During the sprinting session during the warm-up period before the game, the hamstring went again. The question was posed, is Bobby to be replaced? 'No way,' said Heffernan. 'He plays.' And Bobby Doyle did, and served up a brilliant performance with his off the ball running and his ability to create scoring chances for his colleagues. Defences rarely get the credit they deserve on the occasion of major matches: they are very much taken for granted while forwards are rhapsodised about their scoring prowess. But the display of the Dublin defenders in capturing the Sam Maguire in 1976 bore little relationship to the harsh criticism meted out to them following the team's defeat in 1975.

The significance of it is realised when you contrast the statistics of the 1976 championship with those of the previous year. When Dublin lost the title in 1975, the defence conceded 12 goals and 45 points over five games. Look at the difference in 1976: only a total of 1–45 was totted up against Dublin in the five-match championship. This was a points aggregate of only 48 compared with 81 in the previous championship. Even among the statistics there was evidence before the All-Ireland final of the new stability in the Dublin defence, if we had only recognised it in time. The new half back line, which only came together for the semi-final against Galway, made a great difference. The outstanding play of Kevin Moran at centre back after appearing in the first round of the championship as centre forward against Longford, the steadiness of Tommy Drumm on the right and the no-nonsense approach of the hard grafting Pat O'Neill on the left, constituted a line of immense solidarity.

Yet these were not the only factors. The work of Seán Doherty could not be underestimated. In 1976 he regained the confidence that had made him such a bulwark two years earlier, and he played with zest and self-assurance. Robbie Kelleher was steadiness personified. Gay O'Driscoll, who seemed to relish the toughest pressure, showed a new measure of enterprise even at that stage of his career. The man in the last line of that

defence — goalkeeper Paddy Cullen — must be paid a very special tribute. He appeared to scorn the passage of time and his saves in the 1976 final emphasised his right to be recognised as the outstanding keeper in the game. With such a goalkeeper, along with the alert and inflexible defence he had before him, Dublin were bound to regain the title.

The 1976 All-Ireland final story would not be complete without a reference to the work of Brian Mullins and Bernard Brogan in the middle of the field. It is an accepted fact that a superiority at midfield is essential if a team is to achieve victory. In 1975 the Dublin midfield enjoyed periods of dominance, but not enough to break the stranglehold exerted by the strong Kerry pairing of Paudie Lynch and Pat McCarthy. One year later it was the turn of Mullins and Brogan. They made sure there was going to be no repeat of that situation. The fact that the Dublin partnership laid down a marker at an early stage proved the inspiration the team needed. The rest is history. It may be no harm to mention that in securing the coveted double of league and championship in 1976, Dublin equalled the feat achieved by the 1958 team. Beating the Kingdom in the Wembley tournament in 1976 completed a notable treble for the Dubs.

The work rate of the forwards must not be forgotten either. Throughout the championship alone, they mounted these totals: Jimmy Keaveney 6-18, Pat Gogarty 2-6, Anton O'Toole 2-5, David Hickey 0-7, Tony Hanahoe and John McCarthy 1-2 each, and Bobby Doyle 0-4. But their part was not confined solely to scores; with clever running, deft passing and excellent team work, they played a major role in bringing back the Sam Maguire cup after its twelve-month sojourn in the Kingdom.

The All-Ireland final victory was suitably celebrated and followed a pattern already laid down with visits to schools and colleges in the city. When the players received a note to be present for a celebration dinner in the Gresham Hotel on 16 October, it was thought that it would bring the year to a successful conclusion. But unknown to the players there was a sting in the tail. Speculation had been mounting for some time prior to the 1976 All-Ireland final that Kevin Heffernan might not be staying on as manager.

It was well known that he wanted to opt out after the 1974 success but was dissuaded from doing so by the county board officials. I knew from chats I had with Kevin that pressure from his workplace was increasing daily. But the greatest pressure stemmed from the manager's job itself. There was simply no let-up in the constant demands which the position entailed. When the players sat down to enjoy their meal in the Gresham, the only talk was that of fundraising for the trip to San Francisco. But Donal Colfer, Lorcan Redmond and Tony Hanahoe knew that the evening was going to end with a spectacular announcement that would subsequently shock the players. Kevin Heffernan rose to say his few words and it was only then that the true significance of the dinner hit home. Kevin was stepping down as team manager. A deadly silence greeted the announcement.

The earlier euphoria was now replaced by a different atmosphere as players rose to say their piece. But Kevin held up his hands for their attention. The noise subsided. The manager was going to have his say. He explained that when he took the job originally in the autumn of 1973, he had set himself a three-year stint in which to bring back All-Ireland glory to the capital city. But when he achieved in one year what he thought would take three, he decided to opt out. He had accomplished his mission. But Dublin chairman Jimmy Gray and the other board officials eventually talked him out of his decision. Three years on, he had his mind made up. He explained to a now silenced room that he had given three years of his life to the position. He could not continue the workload for another year in a job that demanded his personal attention night and day, and hope to serve his employers as well. The players realised there was no way that Kevin could be persuaded to stay on. The board reluctantly accepted his decision, and some time later the position

Jack Lynch, Cardinal Ó Fiaich and Mrs Lynch watching the battle unfold between Dublin and Kerry in the 1976 All-Ireland final at Croke Park.

was offered to Tony Hanahoe, after Donal Colfer and Lorcan Redmond agreed to stay on as selectors.

I have known Kevin Heffernan since we played on Dublin football teams. We live on the same road in Raheny on Dublin's northside. Kevin was a brilliant forward and served Dublin well. When he took over the reins in Dublin he had a dream. He wanted to mould a team that would reflect his thoughts on how Gaelic football should be played. He approached that challenge fully in the knowledge that changes would have to be made in the team make-up. He needed particular players for particular roles. That would mean a lot of hard work to attain the high level of performance he envisaged as the 'Dublin style'. It can be safely stated that Heffernan brought a new dimension to the game of Gaelic football. It meant hard work during training, night and day.

Emphasis was on coaching, perfecting certain ploys which were needed against specific opposition, and he insisted on implementing those gambits during the course of major matches.

He had willing helpers in his co-selectors, Donal Colfer and Lorcan Redmond, a trio that produced two All-Ireland titles in three years. Heffernan was always a pragmatist but was never known to criticise a player publicly on foot of a poor display. It was always done privately and out of earshot. His era with Dublin will go down in history as the 'golden years' of Dublin football, and it will take many years of searching to find a replacement of his calibre. Kevin's character is reflected in the qualities he instilled in Dublin teams. That fierce competitive spirit is readily identifiable in him to this day.

5

Glory and Decline

One of the most unforgettable games of football ever witnessed on the Croke Park sod was undoubtedly the Dublin–Kerry All-Ireland semi-final of 1977. It stood out as the most pulsating, heart-stopping and mind-boggling confrontation ever staged between the great rivals. That semi-final had everything one could ask for: speed of movement, great scores, glorious fielding, memorable combination and team work, and that applied to both teams. Dublin may have survived, but Kerry's challenge justified an award in itself. The official attendance that day was 59,974, the highest at a semi-final

at Croke Park since 71,573 spectators saw Down defeat Kerry in 1961, but that was before semi-finals were televised live.

Dublin 3-12, Kerry 1-13 was the scoreline at the end of one of the best exhibitions of football served up by the two sides since their exciting meeting in the 1976 All-Ireland final clash. Pádraig Puirséal wrote about the game in the *Irish Press* the following day:

'Elvis is gone, but the Dubs live on', announced the most topical of the many blue and white banners on Hill 16. But Tony Hanahoe and his Dubliners are not only alive, they never lived more gloriously than they did at Croke Park yesterday, when they played possibly the most attractive football of their careers to beat Kerry fair and square in one of the best games of football staged at Headquarters in twenty years. If the first half was fast and furious it was only a foretaste of the thrills to come. After the interval two great teams gave us a contest of almost regal splendour with fortunes flaming and fading, and the only regret for the neutral spectator was that one team had to lose.

Deprived of what would have been the wonderful inspiration of a 30-second goal, the champions, trailing right through the first half, took the lead for the first time in the last quarter, saw Kerry snatch back the advantage, levelled once more, fell two points in arrears with little more than six minutes remaining, but came storming back to achieve a sensational and convincing victory. And yet, Dublin missed a sitter right from the throw-in when Bobby Doyle put Jimmy Keaveney clean through, but the veteran full forward, taking extra care to put the ball wide of Kerry goalkeeper Paud O'Mahony, unbelievably sent it past the upright as well.

As the teams warmed to their task, it was Kerry who set the gruelling pace, hunting in droves around midfield but getting little change out of a hard-pressed but rarely over-stretched Dublin defence, in which Robbie Kelleher, four days back from San Francisco, looked invincible. The Kerrymen were three points clear when Brian Mullins, seemingly stung to life after being warned for a personal foul, suddenly became the outstanding figure around midfield. Bernard Brogan soon joined him as Fran Ryder was called ashore. At half-time Kerry led 1-6 to 0-6.

The second half produced moments of real splendour from a football viewpoint, in which both teams shared equally. Yet in that nerve-tingling finish there could be no question at all that Dublin well merited their first semi-final victory over Kerry since 1934, a victory that carried them through to their fourth successive All-Ireland final. Rarely have so many men played so well at one and the same time. Some of the Dublin forays bore the stamp of incredulity. With Croke Park a cauldron of cheering, Doherty repulsed a dangerous Kerry raid, and Robbie Kelleher sent on a clearance to David Hickey, who passed to Hanahoe who placed Brogan. The tall engineer, who a week before was on an oil rig off Cherbourg, raced 30 yards with the ball, hand to toe, almost unchallenged, before flashing the ball to the Kerry net.

One cannot forget Paddy Cullen's marvellous save when Kerry's Seán Walsh, with the Dublin defence drawn out of position, raced in, drew Cullen and flicked the ball over the goalkeeper's head. But Cullen had narrowed the angle so expertly

The 1984 All-Ireland semi-final, Dublin v Tyrone. FROM LEFT TO RIGHT: *Gerry Hargan (Dublin), Brian Mullins (Dublin), P.J. Buckley (Dublin).*

that the ball passed right across the posts and was gratefully intercepted by Kevin Moran.

Unforgettable too were Anton O'Toole's four great points from various angles, Tommy Drumm's blotting out of the threat posed by Pat Spillane (kept scoreless from play), and Pat O'Neill for a wonderfully versatile display in the half back line. All three were excellent, but then where would you leave Robbie Kelleher who had another 'blinder', Mullins who had some unbeatable moments at midfield, and not forgetting the brilliance and craft of Tony Hanahoe and his back-up team of John McCarthy, Bobby Doyle, David Hickey, Jimmy Keaveney and Bernard Brogan in the second half. Gay O'Driscoll and goalie Paddy Cullen produced a consistently high performance of reliability, equally matched by the versatile Kevin Moran who covered very inch of the Croke Park sod. His was a towering display from start to finish.

The 1977 All-Ireland football final

The 1983 Dublin All-Ireland champions. BACK ROW, LEFT TO RIGHT: *Tommy Conroy, Barney Rock, John Caffrey, Gerry Hargan, Joe McNally, John O'Leary, Anton O'Toole, Mick Holden, Ciarán Duff.* FRONT ROW, LEFT TO RIGHT: *Brian Mullins, P.J. Buckley, Tommy Drumm, Pat Canavan, Ray Hazely, Jim Roynane.*

between Dublin and Armagh never reached the high pinnacle of performance served up in the Dublin-Kerry semi-final. There was no hoped-for football miracle and Tony Hanahoe's Dubliners, without ever looking really distressed, retained the Sam Maguire cup and brought the All-Ireland title to the metropolis for the 20th time on a 5-12 to 3-6 scoreline. Though we saw the highest aggregate score ever in a 70-minute final, the biggest total ever recorded by a winning team, and an all-time individual scoring record in a final set by Jimmy Keaveney, there was too wide a margin between the sides to give the encounter the competitive edge it sadly needed.

So for the first time since the early 1920s, Dublin had succeeded in retaining the All-Ireland title, the first time the county had retained the Sam Maguire cup and the first time the same captain (Tony Hanahoe) had stepped up twice to take the coveted trophy. Certainly there could be no more deserving winners than Dublin on that occasion. From goal to full forward they looked like the great champions they were, and their team work, understanding and combination can rarely have been seen to better effect. Captain Hanahoe's main contribution to that particular game was his intelligent running off the ball, while the full forward line of John McCarthy, Jimmy Keaveney and Anton O'Toole was the power house of the division who between them ran up the remarkable total of 5-10, all but two points of the team's tally.

In the process, Keaveney broke by a point the individual scoring record in a football final, the 2-5 achieved by Frankie Stockwell for Galway in 1956. From the date of his come-back outing up to and including the all-Ireland final of 1976 in the Heffernan era, he assisted Dublin to the tune of 22 goals and 221 points in 39 appearances.

For his contribution to the resurgence of Gaelic football in Dublin, Kevin Heffernan was honoured as the Texaco award winner in Gaelic football for 1974. Two years later, Jimmy Keaveney was acclaimed as the Texaco winner of 1976. Dublin players who received All-Star Awards were as follows:

Dublin GAA All-Stars 1974: (6) Paddy Cullen, Seán Doherty, Robbie Kelleher, Paddy Reilly, David Hickey, Jimmy Keaveney.
GAA All-Stars 1975: (3) Gay O'Driscoll, Robbie Kelleher, Anton O'Toole.
GAA All-Stars 1976: (7) Paddy Cullen, Kevin Moran, Brian Mullins, Anton O'Toole, Tony Hanahoe, David Hickey, Bobby Doyle.
GAA All-Stars 1977: (9) Paddy Cullen, Gay O'Driscoll, Robbie Kelleher, Tommy Drumm, Pat O'Neill, Brian Mullins, Anton O'Toole, Bobby Doyle, Jimmy Keaveney.

Dublin captain Tommy Drumm with the Sam Maguire cup after the 1983 All-Ireland final.

Kevin Heffernan watches anxiously from the sideline during the 1983 All-Ireland final.

GAA All-Stars 1978: (3) Robbie Kelleher, Tommy Drumm, Jimmy Keaveney.

GAA All-Stars 1979: (3) Paddy Cullen, Tommy Drumm, Bernard Brogan.

The great rivalry between Dublin and Kerry, especially at All-Ireland level, brought a new dimension to football and the two counties brought the crowds flocking to Croke Park for their epic battles. The emphasis was always on football and rarely did standards fall. The teams respected each other. They were great friends off the field but the keenest of rivals when pitted against each other in the white heat of the championship. From a Dublin perspective Kerry were always the team to beat and laying the Kingdom bogey became almost a way of life with Dublin players. Dublin had the greatest incentive of all — pride, pride in

The 1984 All-Ireland football final. FROM LEFT TO RIGHT: *Mick Spillane (Kerry), Tommy Conroy (Dublin), Paudie O'Shea (Kerry), Sean Walsh (Kerry), Jim Roynane (Dublin), Joe McNally (Dublin).*

Brian Mullins after the 1985 Leinster final.

The 1985 Dublin All-Ireland finalists. BACK ROW, LEFT TO RIGHT: *Tommy Conroy, Barney Rock, John Kearns, Brian Mullins, Ray Hazely, John O'Leary, Gerry Hargan, Ciarán Duff.* FRONT ROW, LEFT TO RIGHT: *Charlie Redmond, Mick Kennedy, Noel McCaffrey, David Synnott, Joe McNally, Pat Canavan, Jim Roynane.*

themselves and pride in their county. They were constantly reminded by the media that while success came their way at All-Ireland level in 1942, 58, 63 and 74, they were open to the age-old charge, 'Ah, yes, but you didn't beat Kerry after all.' In 1976, as I walked across the Croke Park pitch with selector Lorcan Redmond after Dublin's National League victory over Derry, Lorcan commented: 'This is beyond doubt the best Dublin team ever.' It was a sincere tribute from a man who had been part of Dublin's football revolution. When one fastens the tag 'best' as a descriptive term on a team, it denotes a finality, a superlative which cannot be bettered, irrespective of what may emerge in the years to come.

Success in both All-Ireland and National League in the one year is a rare accomplishment. That was achieved in 1976 when they reversed their 1975 form by winning the two finals they had lost the previous year. Never before in the history

The 1987 National Football League semi-final at O'Moore Park, Portlaoise. Ciarán Duff (Dublin) kicks the ball over the outstretched hands of Frank Broderick (Galway).

of Dublin teams had such an amalgamation of diverse talents achieved such a unity of purpose. That in itself is the hallmark of greatness. And it is a tribute to the work of the selectors, Kevin Heffernan, Lorcan Redmond and Donal Colfer. (It is not often mentioned that Dublin contested nine All-Ireland senior football finals in the 15 years under that management team, winning four, 1974, 76, 77 and 83.)

There is something unique about Dublin-Galway All-Ireland senior football championship meetings. I have seen them all since I watched Galway beat Kerry in my first All-Ireland football final in 1938. Rarely during that period have I witnessed a game between the two counties which would have satisfied the football purist. For some unknown reason, standards dropped and a more physical element was introduced to spoil it as a contest. Such was the case in the 1983 All-Ireland final between the two counties. This final will be remembered as the one in which 12 Dubliners overcame the challenge of 14 Galwaymen with a brave back-to-the-wall second half showing by Dublin which brought the county 'of age' with a 21st All-Ireland senior title.

This was a remarkable achievement by the Dubs — all the more so as they had to play against a gale force wind in the second

The 1987 National Football League final, Dublin v Kerry. Final instructions from the manager Gerry McCaul to Dublin players Glen O'Neill, Noel McCaffrey and Gerry Hargan.

The 1987 National Football League semi-final at Portlaoise. Dublin player Dave Synnott (WITH HIS BACK TO THE CAMERA) *awaits the outcome of this tussle.*

Brian Mullins about to lay off the ball to a forward.

half. The Leinster champions, playing their best football of the game during that period, suffered a set-back in the form of a Galway goal after 15 minutes, but held out for a well-deserved win.

Dublin midfielder Brian Mullins was dismissed by the referee nine minutes before half-time. Four minutes later Dublin left corner back Ray Hazely and Galway right corner forward Tomas Tierney were harshly sent off for a minor incident. The second half was only five minutes old when Kieran Duff, Dublin's left half forward, received his marching orders. At that stage Dublin led by six points after turning over at the break 1-5, 0-2 in front, but their prospects of winning looked decidedly bleak after Duff's dismissal. However, with a display of true grit seldom if ever seen at GAA headquarters, the Liffeysiders rose to the challenge in magnificent fashion.

The motivator and star of the Dublin rally was undoubtedly the majestic Pat Canavan at right half back. He broke the hearts of the Galway attack with a display that ranked with the best ever by a defender in the cauldron of an All-Ireland final. He served up football of the highest standard and also found time to set his own forward division into action. His was a five-star show that proved influential in orchestrating the brave Dublin effort, and one that understandably earned the St Vincent's club man the 'man of the match' award.

When the going was toughest, Canavan, Gerry Hargan, Tommy Drumm, a true captain leading by example in defence, Barney Rock and Anton O'Toole in attack, never spared themselves. Although Galway, who were attempting to close a gap of 17 years since their last title win, had no outstanding player, Johnny Hughes in defence, Barry Brennan and Stephen Joyce in attack were best. It was a pity the game turned into a bad-tempered, bruising affair with a surfeit of frees after a bright opening.

I hope I haven't been too dismissive of the 1983 final. Suffice to say that Dublin's 'coming of age' was not the celebration

The 1985 All-Ireland semi-final. FROM LEFT TO RIGHT: *Kevin McStay (Mayo), Dave Synnott (Dublin), Eugene McHale (Mayo).*

party that many of their most committed supporters had expected. On reflection, the 1983 final was overshadowed by memories of the drawn and replayed All-Ireland semi-final against Cork. The drawn game at Croke Park had attracted an attendance of 49,773. The deepest and most emotional roar ever heard at Croke Park for one single goal in football erupted when Barney Rock netted the equaliser for Dublin in the closing minutes. Rock was in the right place at the right time when Brian Mullins, with time ticking away, kept his head when he found himself in possession and waited that vital few seconds before parting with the ball to Ray Hazely, coming up in an overlapping run on the left wing. His centre across the Cork goal-mouth caught the Leesiders' defence flat footed. Barney Rock snapped it up to stab the ball home at the Railway end to become 'king of the Hill' in an electrifying and never to be forgotten moment.

'Molly Malone' and the Hill came to Pairc Uí Chaoimh for the replay, played out on a wonderful sunny day before an attendance of 43,438. It was a unique occasion, brimful of colour and singing, of synchronised chanting and tremendous atmosphere. From the buzz around the ground it was evident that this was no ordinary confrontation, but the kind only the Dubs can create, especially when in contention against Cork or Kerry. The Dublin selectors ordered the team and the substitutes to sit out on the sideline to get a feel for the atmosphere. The captain Tommy Drumm told me a few days after the match, that the sight of 10,000 Dublin fans bedecked in blue favours with waving flags and banners was awesome. 'I said to some of the players sitting with me, "Jesus, lads, we cannot let those fans down. Listen to them."' They took over the Blackrock end of the stadium which someone christened 'Hill 17'.

Dublin were a goal up inside three minutes when Barney Rock was pulled down and Brian Mullins converted the penalty. Dublin led 1-7 to 0-5 at half-time after having played against the wind. Cork had two goals from Dave Barry in the second half, but Dublin were flying on all cylinders. Goals from Ciarán Duff, Barney Rock, and a cheeky goal from Joe McNally had the 'Hill 17' supporters roaring their heads off. When it was all over, Brian Mullins, covered in sweat after a lion-hearted display, walked over to 'Hill 17' with the rest of the Dublin players, and with arms uplifted in a gesture of triumph, thanked the supporters at the Blackrock end of the ground for the special support they had given them on the day.

It goes without saying that the All-Ireland senior football championship continues to be by far the most popular spectator sport on this island. But it can also be said that in recent years, because of the new format of the hurling championship introduced in 1997, the

The 1985 All-Ireland semi-final, Dublin v Mayo. Ciarán Duff (Dublin) challenged by Martin Carney and John Finn (Mayo).

national game of hurling is fast catching up. Attendances at All-Ireland hurling semi-finals and finals are growing. Indeed a stage has now been reached where the gap between the attendances at the two is often less than 1,000 out of some 65,000 attending each game. In the 20-year period from 1980 to 1999, 22 football finals were played, those for 1988 and 1996 going to replays. Three salient points emerge from an analysis of the list of winners and contestants for the Sam Maguire cup.

These are: the continued dominance well into the 1980s of Kerry football, its

Charlie Redmond (Dublin) in full flight.

The 1987 National Football League semi-final at Portlaoise, Dublin v Galway. Dublin players Dave Synnott (5) and Gerry Hargan look on as Galway player Tomás Tierney kicks the ball.

eclipse in the early 1990s by Ulster football and, with the solitary exception of Galway in 1998 and 2000, the failure of any Connacht county to bring the Sam Maguire trophy across the Shannon. How radically the scene has changed in Gaelic football in the past 17 years (1987 to 2004) can perhaps be best judged from two facts: that Kerry's name has been etched on the Sam Maguire cup only three times (1997, 2000 and 2004) in that period; and similarly that the name of Dublin (Kerry's

main rival in the 1970s) has only once been added (in 1995) in the same period.

Contrariwise, in the same 17-year period, Ulster counties have won the coveted trophy on six occasions: Down (1991, 94), Donegal (1992), Armagh (2002), and Tyrone (2003). Tyrone, Derry Armagh and Donegal are first-time winners to date.

No brief review of Gaelic football would be complete without a reference to the extraordinary Dublin-Meath epic

Dublin captain Gerry Hargan with the National Football League cup of 1987. GAA President Michael Loftus addresses the crowd.

The 1988 National Football League final. Mick Kennedy (Dublin) showing the pressure as he clears the ball to safety.

1988 National Football League finalists, Meath. BACK ROW, LEFT TO RIGHT: *Colm O'Rourke, Mick Lyons, Gerry McEntee, Michael McQuillan, Martin O'Connell, Liam Hayes, David Beggy.* FRONT ROW, LEFT TO RIGHT: *P.J. Gillic, Terry Ferguson, Colm Coyle, Bernard Flynn, Robbie O'Malley, Padraig Lyons, Liam Harnan, Kevin Foley.*

Meath player Colm O'Rourke shoots forward.

The 1991 National Football League final, Dublin v Kildare. Tommy Carr (Dublin) goes for the ball between Kildare players Bill Lex (7) and John Crofton.

Dublin footballer and fireman Charlie Redmond.

After the Dublin v Kildare National Football League final 1991, Tommy Carr shows off the League trophy to the fans on Hill 16 as Vinny Murphy celebrates in the background.

Colm O'Rourke and Mick Kennedy of Dublin both go to ground as they battle for possession in the 1990 Dublin v Meath Leinster football final.

The Artane Boys Band entertaining Hill 16 fans.

Tommy Dowd of Meath challenges Dublin keeper John O'Leary for possession in the 1991 Leinster football championship.

Mick Galvin celebrates scoring a vital goal for Dublin in the 1991 Leinster football championship.

Jack Sheedy rattles the back of the net as he scores a goal for Dublin in the 1991 Leinster championship.

Keith Barr misses a penalty for Dublin in the Leinster championship replay in 1991.

More action from the 1991 Dublin v Meath championship replay. Referee Tommy Howard throws in the ball to the eager Paul Bealin of Dublin and Liam Hayes and P.J. Gillic of Meath.

In the 1992 Dublin v Clare All-Ireland football semi-final, Paul Curran and Paul Bealin of Dublin and Tom Morrissey of Clare jump together for a high ball.

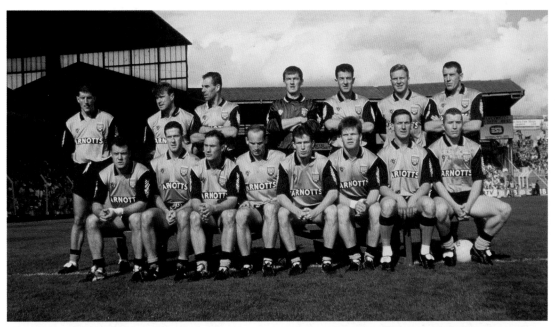

The 1992 Dublin All-Ireland finalists v Donegal. BACK ROW, LEFT TO RIGHT: *Mick Galvin, Charlie Redmond, Dave Foran, John O'Leary, Gerry Hargan, Keith Barr, Jack Sheedy.* FRONT ROW, LEFT TO RIGHT: *Vinnie Murphy, Paul Clarke, Paul Curran, Tommy Carr, Niall Guiden, Dessie Farrell, Mick Deegan, Eamon Heery.*

Loyal Dublin fans on the Hill give vent to their feelings.

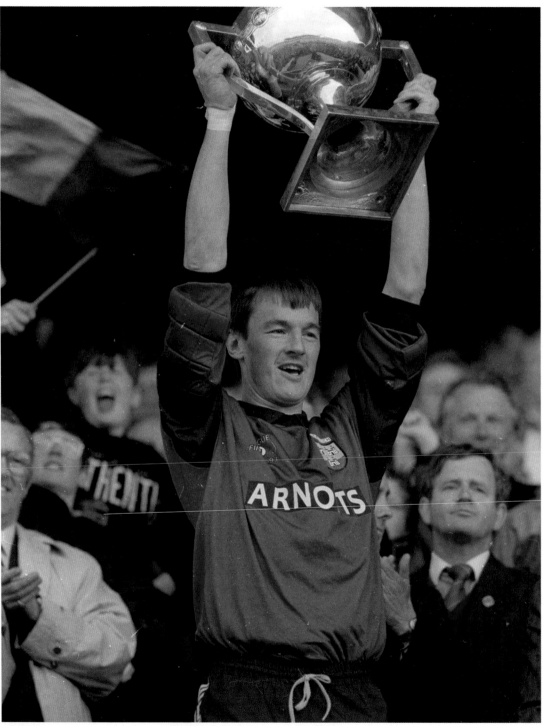

John O'Leary celebrates victory after Dublin beat Donegal in the 1993 National Football League final.

Vinny Murphy of Dublin gets sent off in
the 1993 Leinster football final.

A disappointed Jason Sherlock after the
1996 Leinster final v Meath.

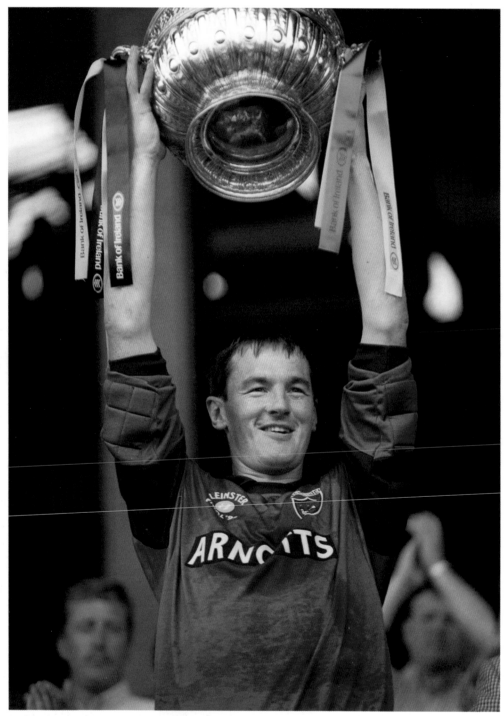

John O'Leary lifts the cup as Dublin win the 1994 Leinster football final.

four-game marathon in 1991. Rivalry between the two counties has built up over the years, but nowhere more so than in that spectacular first round Leinster championship clash of the two counties before an attendance of 51,000. The fourth game, played on Saturday, 6 July, before an official attendance of 61,543 at Croke Park, produced a climax that must rank among the most dramatic and emotionally charged matches in football history.

Into the closing stages of the latter the Dublin fans on the Hill were dancing with joy in anticipation of yet another defeat of their great rivals. Dublin were four points clear with six minutes remaining. Fifteen minutes into the second half the scoreboard had read Dublin 0-12, Meath 0-6. But then came that closing burst by Meath when Kevin Foley scored a killer goal that silenced the Hill. Two minutes remained when, after Brian Stafford had reduced the deficit to three points, Martin O'Connell gained possession near his own end line and released the ball to Mick Lyons. He placed Liam Harnan who passed to Colm O'Rourke. O'Rourke distributed via Foley, P.J. Gillic and Tommy Dowd before collecting again and finding Foley, who had ranged up from the half back line to join in that final do or die assault, to crack the ball home. The teams were level. Before Dublin had time to regroup, Meath midfielder Liam Hayes caught John O'Leary's kick-out, raced away on a solo run, passed to Gillic and he in turn placed Dave Beggy who right footed the ball over the Dublin crossbar. Dublin's Jack Sheedy had one last chance of snatching a draw, but his effort from a long-distance free went wide of the posts. Here were the final scores:

First game: 2 June Dublin 1-12, Meath 1-12
Attendance 51, 144
Replay 1: 9 June Dublin 1-11, Meath 1-11
(after 30 mins extra time)
Attendance 60,960
Replay 2: 23 June Dublin 1-14, Meath 2-11
(after 30 mins extra time)
Attendance 63,730
Replay 3: 6 July Meath 2-10, Dublin 0-15
Attendance 61,543

Former Dublin star Jimmy Keaveney claimed that the turning point in that third replay was Keith Barr's missed penalty eight minutes from the end. Dublin were leading by three points and he was adamant that had Barr been instructed to take a point at the time by the team mentors, Meath's task would have been a different story. But in fairness to Keith Barr he was unfairly pressured in his run-up to the ball by Meath's Mick Lyons, who ran alongside Barr as he was taking the spot kick. A retaken penalty should have been ordered by the referee at the time. That was the view of a number of referees present on that occasion.

Some of the statistics of this epic series are of interest. Meath accumulated a gross score of 6-44 (62 points), Dublin 3-52 (61 points). The total gate receipts amounted to £1,055,000 and the total attendance was over 240,000. Leinster provincial secretary Michael Delaney was a very happy GAA official and said after the last match that it constituted not alone a record for a first-round Leinster championship game, but for any sequence of championship games between two teams in GAA history.

Two years on from that climactic game in 1991 Meath and Dublin faced each other in the Leinster championship semi-final of 1993. The attendance was 63,164. This was a poor game in contrast to the excitement of the 1991 series of matches. Dublin won with Charlie Redmond the top scorer with 1-7. Jack Sheedy put the issue beyond doubt when he fired over a great point from 45 yards in injury time. That win buried the Meath hoodoo which had afflicted Dublin for so long.

In every decade of the past half-century or so, a county with little or no record of provincial honours suddenly rises to the top in Gaelic football. In the 1930s it was Laois; in the 1940s it was Roscommon. Three counties performed this feat in football championships of the past 20 years, Clare in 1992, Leitrim in 1994 and Kildare in 1998. The Munster county had been close to success before, but in 1992 it won the provincial title for the first time in 75 years by defeating Kerry. Facing Dublin in the All-Ireland semi-final, Clare were only three points down at the interval and cut this to one in the last quarter before the Dubs surged ahead to win by five points (3-14 to 2-12) before an attendance of 58,000.

Two years later Leitrim defeated Mayo (0-12 to 0-10) to take the Connacht title for the first time in 67 years. Like Clare it was unlucky to be drawn against Dublin in the All-Ireland semi-final, going down by double scores (3-15 to 1-9) to a Dublin team that failed to break Ulster's three-year grip on the Sam Maguire cup, Down winning by two points. Finally after several near misses Kildare in 1998 won in Leinster for the first time since 1956, and although losing to Galway in the All-Ireland final by four points, seemed destined to stay at or near the top in Leinster for some time to come. Some other counties which appear capable of major titles in the years ahead are Laois, Wexford, Limerick and Fermanagh. Only time (and the proper management structures) will tell.

In hurling, the past two decades have brought a new look to the national game. In the 1980s two counties (Galway and

Barry Breen of Down tackles Vinny Murphy of Dublin in the 1994 All-Ireland football final.

The 1995 All-Ireland semi-final, Dublin v Cork. FROM LEFT TO RIGHT: *Paddy Moran (Dublin), John O'Leary (Dublin), Colin Corkery (Cork).*

Jason Sherlock scores a goal in the 1995 All-Ireland football final against Tyrone.

Winners of the 1995 All-Ireland football final, Paul Curran and John O'Leary of Dublin hold aloft the Sam Maguire.

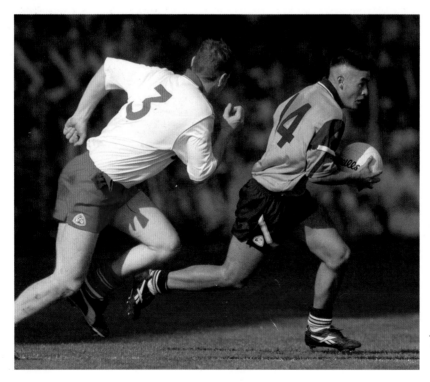

Jason Sherlock pursued by Chris Lawn of Tyrone in the 1995 All-Ireland final.

Photographers take pictures of the 1995 All-Ireland Dublin team. BACK ROW, LEFT TO RIGHT: *Paul Clarke, Mick Galvin, Ciaran Walsh, Paul Bealin, Brian Stynes, Paddy Moran, Keith Barr.* FRONT ROW, LEFT TO RIGHT: *Jason Sherlock, Jim Gavin, Dessie Farrell, Paul Curran, John O'Leary, Keith Galvin, Mick Deegan, Charlie Redmond.*

Mick Deegan and Charlie Redmond with daughter Claire in the Sam Maguire during the 1995 Dublin homecoming.

2000 and the Dublin team form a huddle before a Leinster football championship game at Croke Park.

Paul Curran dejected after the Leinster football championship game at Croke Park.

Jason Sherlock of Dublin evades the challenge of Ken Doyle (Kildare) in the 2000 Leinster football final replay.

Kerry keeper Declan O'Keeffe looks back helplessly as Vinny Murphy celebrates his goal in the 2001 All-Ireland quarter-final.

Dublin manager Tommy Carr remonstrates with referee Mick Curley at the 2001 All-Ireland quarter-final v Kerry in Thurles.

A Dublin fan at the 2001 All-Ireland quarter-final in Thurles.

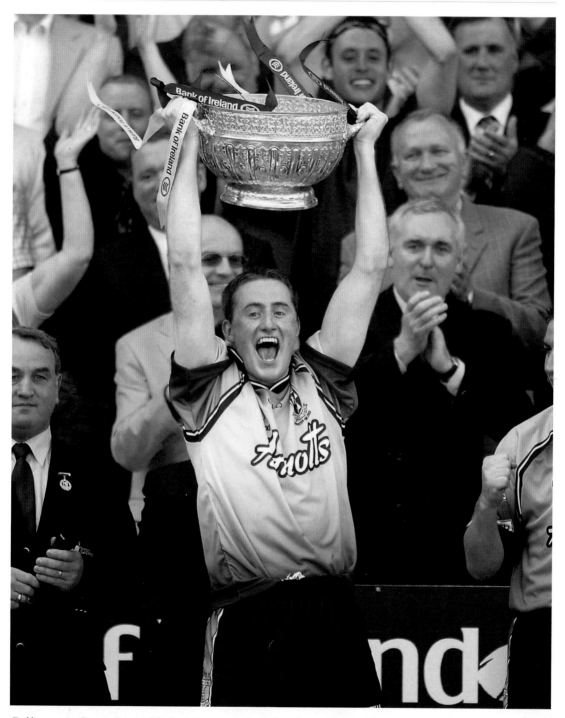

Dublin captain Coman Goggins lifts the Leinster senior football trophy in 2002.

Jason Sherlock celebrates with Dublin fans on Hill 16 after victory in the 2002 Leinster football final.

Darren Magee and Paul Casey of Dublin with the Leinster football trophy after their victory over Kildare in 2002.

Aerial action from the 2002 Dublin v Armagh All-Ireland semi-final.

Fish-eye view of Dublin players Jonathan Magee and Paul Casey running on to the pitch in the 2002 All-Ireland semi-final.

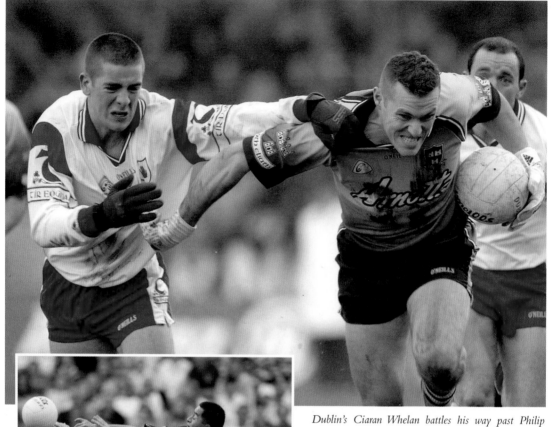

Dublin's Ciaran Whelan battles his way past Philip Jordan of Tyrone in the Allianz National League 2003.

Jason Sherlock of Dublin and Damien Healy of Westmeath tussle for the ball in the 2004 Leinster football championship.

The 2004 All-Ireland quarter-final, Kerry v Dublin. Alan Brogan (Dublin) and Marc Ó Sé (Kerry).

Selector Brian Talty and Dublin manager Tommy Lyons.

Dublin captain Paddy Christie lifts the Leinster senior football trophy in front of celebrating Dublin fans in 2005.

Offaly), both in effect new to senior titles, won senior All-Ireland crowns. The 1990s saw a surge in popularity for the game which is almost certainly linked to the new format of the final stages of the senior and minor championships. The Connacht contender for the McCarthy cup, in effect the only real contender in the province, Galway, contested six of the ten finals of the 1980s and won three of them, more than any other county in the whole decade. Galway's solitary senior hurling title was back in 1923, its only success before 1980 in the 96-year-old history of the GAA. The fact that the three losers to Galway in 1980, 1987 and 1988 were, respectively, Limerick, Kilkenny and Tipperary, all from the traditional heartland of the game, made their achievement all the more impressive.

As RTÉ entered the 1980s, the organisation found itself in a remarkably similar position to that experienced by the young Radio Éireann in the early 1930s. It enjoyed neither the confidence of politicians nor that of the powerful traditional lobbies. In both cases this stemmed from the nature of the financial arrangements that the State imposed on the broadcasting services and the failure of governments to address the issues involved in sustaining services designed to maintain and develop all the dimensions of Irish culture in the face of the flood of influence from abroad. RTÉ in the 1980s, however, had a measure of autonomy that had been wholly denied to its predecessor in the 1930s. It proved successful both in its capacity to attain profitability and in the premise on which this had to be based: that is, in its capacity to achieve a high audience share.

Neither of these achievements, however, protected RTÉ from the designs of unsympathetic, disaffected politicians, who were increasingly determined to provide directly competitive, alternative commercial services. When these almost immediately proved non-viable, the politicians moved once again to attack RTÉ by skimming off its profits to subsidise its rivals. The rhetoric used to justify these political actions was that the new services would provide greater choice for viewers and listeners.

Within RTÉ there was a conviction that the application of section 31 of the Broadcasting Act was inhibiting news and current affairs broadcasting. While this was undoubtedly the case, there would appear to have been deeper forces at work achieving a somewhat similar effect in newspapers, where there was no external censorship. In 1980/81 the sequence of hunger strikes in Northern Ireland by incarcerated members of the Provisional IRA won an unparalleled degree of attention from all the media in Ireland and in the United Kingdom. A remarkable

View from the Hill. A general view of the action from Hill 16 in the Dublin v Tyrone football quarter-final.

wave of sympathy for the strikers was engendered even among moderate nationalists, and perhaps an equal and opposite reaction among those who favoured Northern Ireland's union with Britain. The evidence suggests that this episode was to prove the last point at which the mass media exerted a powerful influence on their various publics through the coverage of the Northern Ireland crisis. Thereafter, the coverage and consequential influence was to decline. There was also a marked contraction in the number of journalists and photographers assigned to the North.

Dublin took nine years to reach their next All-Ireland senior football final, in 1992, when their opponents were Donegal. The Dublin selection board had changed with Paddy Cullen as manager, and Pat O'Neill, Jim Brogan, Fran Ryder and Bobby Doyle as selectors. Donegal had never won an All-Ireland senior championship semi-final until they overcame Mayo in the penultimate stage of the 1992 series. That was a marvellous boost for Donegal going into their first All-Ireland final.

Dublin, on the other hand, had never been beaten by an Ulster team in the All-Ireland championship and naturally they were firm favourites to collect the Sam Maguire cup. But they came up against a Donegal team who played out of their skins on the day and deservedly captured the coveted honours by 0-18 to 0-14. It was claimed that a missed penalty by Charlie Redmond in the ninth minute was to prove the team's undoing, but the fact remained that Donegal imposed their will on the exchanges and blotted out the Dublin danger men. Dublin could not close a gaping hole in the centre of defence as the Donegal forwards ran riot against them. Free taker Manus Boyle took 'man of the match' award, while Martin McHugh had a dream All-Ireland final day. Indeed, Donegal had a nucleus down the middle that Dublin could not match. The plain fact of the matter was that Donegal came, saw and conquered a Dublin team which was never allowed to dictate the flow of play.

There was some recompense for Dublin when the two counties met again in the 1992/93 National League final. Paddy Cullen, very unhappy with the Dublin performance in the 1992 final, had opted out, and Pat O'Neill took over the manager's job. An attendance of 59,000 came to Croke Park for the replay after the teams had finished 0-9 each. Donegal's record of having gone unbeaten in 16 competitive games came to a swift end as a fiery Dublin team captured the honours 0-10 to 0-6. Dublin had Tommy Carr sent off after just five minutes from the start, but the team rose to the challenge to claim a sweet success for captain John O'Leary — ten years on from that day in 1983

A young Dublin fan cheers on his team in the 2005 football quarter-finals.

when he was one of the 'defiant dozen' that beat Galway in the All-Ireland final.

Captain in 1976 and 1977, Tony Hanahoe said of the league success against Donegal: 'A heroic victory for 14 men. I know I said that I thought Dublin had played some of their best football in the drawn game a week ago, but I have to say that yesterday they were superb. It was the best display by a Dublin team that I have seen in years.' The selectors, Dr Pat O'Neill, Jim Brogan, Fran Ryder and Bobby Doyle, were relieved and delighted to come away with a valuable National League title.

Dublin still remain Kerry's closest challengers on the All-Ireland football honours roll with 22 championship titles. Dublin also hold a unique record of winning at least one All-Ireland title in every decade over a span of 50 years from 1942 to the advent of the 1990s. So, a lot was at stake when Dublin trotted out against Tyrone in 1995 at Croke Park on 17 September before an attendance of 65,092. Dublin was bridging a gap of 12 years since their last success in 1983. It was inconceivable that they would allow the last decade to pass before the new millennium without maintaining that proud record and gaining their 22nd title.

The galling four-point defeat at the hands of Donegal still rankled. There had to be atonement too for the one-point defeat at the hands of Derry in the 1993 All-Ireland semi-final, not forgetting the two-point failure against Down in the 1994 final. But Dublin had at least an extra incentive in 1995 when challenged by Tyrone, who were hell bent on chalking up a fifth in a row run of Ulster successes at All-Ireland final level, Down having won in 1991 as well. All in all, it was a very tense occasion for the Dubs under the management of Dr Pat O'Neill and his selectors, Jim Brogan, Bobby Doyle and Fran Ryder. Never was any Dublin team better prepared. Never was a team subjected to such a physically demanding fitness programme as that Dublin team. O'Neill had laid down the law and demanded discipline of the highest degree, and got it.

Ryder and Doyle's training sessions were awesome, and one wondered if the human frame could stand up to the programme they had drawn up. It did and it was to pay off in many ways in that 1995 contest. Facing another Ulster championship-winning side posed a major challenge and the Dubs were well and truly geared for all contingencies. The team was captained by John O'Leary, who had starred between the posts when 'Sam' was brought back to the capital in 1983. Tommy Drumm, who captained the successful 'defiant dozen' in that epic win, and played a major role in it, was very impressed with the preparations for the Tyrone clash. 'I never thought they could lose even when Charlie Redmond was sent off in the second half. The team seemed to find inspiration in adversity, bolstered by sheer grit and determination. They had men out there who had played their hearts out and were not prepared to buckle at any cost.' Charlie Redmond's sending off for alleged head-butting could well have cost Dublin the match. The incident came after 46 minutes and it led to some confusion for a time. The referee Paddy Russell (Tipperary) called Redmond aside and spoke to him, and the spectators believed he had ordered the Dublin man to the sideline. Redmond took a couple of steps towards the line, but as play resumed he remained on the pitch. Two minutes later, however, the referee, after consultation with a linesman, again spoke to Redmond, who then went off.

Dublin led by 1-8 to 0-9 nine minutes into the second half after leading by 1-8 to 0-6 at the interval. The Dublin goal, the only one in the game, was masterminded by the cult figure on the team, Jason Sherlock. The Dublin fans on Hill 16 had really taken him to their hearts on the day he unleashed his cracker of a goal against Cork in the All-Ireland semi-final. He became an integral part of the Dublin team following his displays in the Leinster championship. The ability to create scoring chances was one of his great traits. In the All-Ireland final against Tyrone, he opened the way for the crucial goal that won the title for Dublin. They were a point ahead, 0-6 to 0-5 in the 25th minute of the first half, when a long through ball

from Paul Clarke caught the Tyrone backs by surprise. Sherlock ran on to the ball at the Canal end. The Tyrone goalkeeper Finbarr McConnell, realising the danger, sped out in a race for the ball with Sherlock. It was a fifty fifty ball, but Sherlock to his eternal credit did not shy away from a situation where he ran the risk of a possible leg injury. He got his foot to the ball before McConnell, touching it on, and the in-rushing Charlie Redmond cracked it to an empty net. Paul Curran added a quick point and put the Dubs in a commanding 1-7 to 0-5 lead.

Dublin still led 1-9 to 0-9, nine minutes into the second half, but there were no more scores for 22 minutes until Peter Canavan pointed a free. Tyrone put on the pressure in rare style in the closing minutes and further points from marksman Canavan from frees left just the minimum margin between the teams as the game reached its final moments. Canavan, star of the losing side with his 11 points (10 from frees), gained possession in front of the Dublin posts but was tackled. He managed to scoop the ball into the hands of Seán McLoughlin, who kicked it over for the levelling point. But referee Paddy Russell had blown for a Dublin free, deeming that Canavan had touched the ball illegally on the ground before parting with it to McLoughlin. The final whistle went with Dublin capturing the elusive All-Ireland crown.

While Tyrone bemoaned the disallowed

McLoughlin point, it must be said that the Ulster champions failed to utilise the advantage of playing against Dublin with an extra man for the last 24 minutes of the match. When asked why he got himself sidelined in an incident in front of the Cusack stand, Redmond said: 'Someone came down on top of me with an elbow and a knee and it hurt. I stupidly reacted and should have kept my head. I regretted it afterwards.'

Dublin's 'man of the match' was easily Paul Curran. He gave the most polished display of his life on that particular day. He dominated the whole right-hand side of the field, and his solo running and directional placing of the ball which produced a number of scores brought an immediate response from the fans on the Hill. It was a powerful exhibition of controlled and purposeful football which Tyrone failed to offset. He inspired the men around him, Keith Barr in the centre of the defence and Mick Deegan on the left, and they responded. The proof lay in the fact that the Tyrone half forward line was held scoreless from play.

Little behind on the honours roll was Dessie Farrell. He revelled in his role in the half line of attack, displaying artistry on and off the ball, finishing up with four marvellous points. Paul Clarke and Paul Bealin ruled the roost in the centre of the field, especially during spells in the second half when Tyrone mounted pressure. A special mention is due for Pat Gilroy, who was called into the action in the last 20 minutes of the match. He too played his part in the result.

The final whistle must have come like sweet music for the Dublin selectors, Pat O'Neill, Jim Brogan, Fran Ryder and Bobby Doyle. They shouldered a major responsibility, not alone in the team's preparations, but in the general make-up of the side. The victory they fashioned broke a losing spell in the All-Ireland final going back to 1983. It took a lot of hard grind to adopt a containment policy after Charlie Redmond was sent off. Thankfully, the level of fitness achieved for the occasion stood to Dublin, and the off the ball running created the important and vital scores. It was to be Dublin's only All-Ireland crown in the 1990s.

We are into the sixth year of the 2000s, which means that Dublin have four years left to secure a 23rd All-Ireland football crown to ensure that the record of achieving an All-Ireland success in every decade is accomplished. Is that a tall order? I hardly think so.

Appendix 1

Dublin Football Titles

ALL-IRELAND SENIOR CHAMPIONSHIP (22)
Teams 21 a side (goal outweighed any
number of points)
1891 Dublin (Young Irelands) beat
Cork (Clondrohid) 2-1 to 1-9

TEAMS REDUCED TO 17 A SIDE (GOAL MADE
EQUAL TO 5 POINTS FROM 1892)
1892 At the annual congress county
champions were granted permission
to select players from other clubs
within the county. No Ulster
representatives. Dublin (Young
Irelands) beat Kerry (Laune Rangers)
1-4 to 0-3
1894 Unfinished. Dublin awarded title
(Dublin 0-5 Cork 1-2)

GOAL MADE EQUAL TO 3 POINTS FROM 1896
AND THE PARALLELOGRAM INTRODUCED
1897 Dublin (Kickhams) beat Cork
(Dunmanway) 2-6 to 0-2
1898 Dublin (Geraldines) beat
Waterford (Erin's Hope) 2-8 to 0-4
1899 Dublin (Geraldines) beat Cork
(Nils) 1-10 to 0-6
1901 Dublin (Isle of the Sea) beat
London (Hibernians) 0-14 to 0-2
1902 Dublin (Bray Emmetts) beat
London (Hibernians) 2-8 to 0-4

1906 Dublin (Kickhams) beat Cork
(Fermoy) 0-5 to 0-4
1907 Dublin (Kickhams) beat Cork
(Lees) 0-6 to 0-2
1908 Dublin (Geraldines) beat London
(Hibernians) 1-10 to 0-4

TEAMS REDUCED TO 15 A SIDE FROM 1913
1921 Dublin (St Mary's) beat Mayo
(Stephenites) 1-9 to 0-2
1922 Dublin (O'Tooles) beat Galway
(Ballinasloe) 0-6 to 0-4
1923 Dublin beat Kerry 1-5 to 1-3
1942 Dublin beat Galway 1-10 to 1-8
1958 Dublin beat Derry 2-12 to 1-9
1963 Dublin beat Galway 1-9 to 0-10

FIRST 80-MINUTES FINAL WAS INTRODUCED
IN 1970
1974 Dublin beat Galway 0-14 to 1-6

FIRST 70-MINUTES FINAL WAS INTRODUCED
IN 1975
1976 Dublin beat Kerry 3-8 to 0-10
1977 Dublin beat Armagh 5-12 to 3-6
1983 Dublin beat Galway 1-10 to 1-8
1995 Dublin beat Tyrone 1-10 to 0-12

MINOR FOOTBALL CHAMPIONSHIP (10)
1930, 45, 54, 55, 56, 58, 59, 74, 81, 93

Appendix 2

Dublin Hurling Titles

ALL-IRELAND SENIOR CHAMPIONSHIP (6)
1889 beat Clare 5-1 to 1-6
1917 beat Tipperary 5-4 to 4-2
1920 beat Cork 4-9 to 4-3
1924 beat Galway 5-3 to 2-6
1927 beat Cork 4-8 to 1-3
1938 beat Waterford 2-5 to 1-6

ALL-IRELAND MINOR (4)
1945 beat Tipperary 3-14 to 4-6
1946 beat Tipperary 1-6 to 0-7
1954 beat Tipperary 2-7 to 2-3
1965 beat Limerick 4-10 to 2-7

ALL-IRELAND JUNIOR (3)
1932 beat London 8-4 to 2-0
1937 beat London 7-8 to 3-6
1952 beat London 3-4 to 2-6

NATIONAL LEAGUE (2)
1929 beat Cork 7-4 to 5-5
1939 beat Waterford 1-8 to 1-4

OIREACHTAS HURLING TOURNAMENT (2)
1944 beat Galway 6-6 to 3-6
1948 beat Waterford 3-6 to 2-6

OIREACHTAS FOOTBALL TOURNAMENT 1941–43 (2)
1941 beat Kildare 1-8 to 1-5
(after replay)
1942 beat Cavan 1-6 to 1-3
(Dublin are the only county to have won Oireachtas medals in hurling and football)

WALSH CUP (3)
1930, 64, 66

KEHOE CUP (1)
1981

CAMOGIE (26)
1932, 33, 37, 38, 1942–44, 1948–55, 1957–66, 1984

ALL-IRELAND UNDER 21 (1)
2003

O'BYRNE CUP (LEINSTER) (5)
1956, 58, 60, 66, 69

Bibliography

PRINCIPAL SOURCES
Frankie Byrne NT (former Meath footballer)
Ann Cleary
Sean Coyne, librarian, and staff, Raheny Library
Eoin McCann
Con Martin (international footballer)
The National Library of Ireland
Andrew O'Brien, librarian, and staff, Pearse Street Library
Mervyn O'Driscoll (lecturer in Modern History, UCC)
Tom Woulfe
Jimmy Wren (historian)

De Búrca, Marcus, *The GAA — A History*, Gill & Macmillan, 2000 (paperback edition).
Cronin, Mike, *A History of Ireland*, Palgrave, 2002.
Donnelly, Paddy, *Cumann Iomáine agus Peile (Naomh Uinsionn, 1931–81): A Brief History*.
Dunne, Mick and Maurice Quinn, *Michael O'Hehir. My Life and Times*, Blackwater Press.
Fullam, Brendan, *Giants of the Ash*, Wolfhound, 1991.
Fullam, Brendan, *The Final Whistle: More Unusual GAA Stories*, 2000.
Hill, J. R. (ed.), *A New History of Ireland*, vol. 7, Oxford University Press, 2004.
Keogh, Dermot and Mervyn O'Driscoll (eds), *Ireland in World War Two: Neutrality and Survival*, Mercier Press, 2004.
Litton, Helen, *World War II Years: The Irish Emergency: An Illustrated History*, Wolfhound Press, 2001.
O'Shea, John, *The Book of the Dubs*, City View Press Ltd.
Puirséal, Pádraig, *The GAA in Its Time*. Pub. by Mary Purcell and family.
Ryall, Tom, *Leinster GAA Council 1900–2000: A History*. Pub. by Leinster Council GAA.
Smith, Raymond (ed.), *Complete Handbook of Gaelic Games*, Dublin: DBA Publications, 2006.
Smith, Raymond, *The Football Immortals*, Aherlow Publishers, 1988.
Ó Ceallacháin, Seán Óg, *His Own Story*, Brophy Books, 1988.
Ó Ceallacháin, Seán Óg, *My Greatest Sporting Memory*, Calmac Publishing, 2000.

Index

(NOTE: PAGE NUMBERS IN ITALICS REFER TO ILLUSTRATIONS)